PRAISE FOR
THE TOOLS OF ARGUMENT

"In his new book _The Tools of Argument: How the Best Lawyers Think, Argue, and Win_, Professor Joel Trachtman lays out the many intricacies related to how lawyers frame arguments. It is a masterly treatment of a complex and compelling set of issues. There is much to learn here, both for the experienced practitioner and for the novice to the field."

— James R. Silkenat, President,
American Bar Association (2012-13)
and Partner, Sullivan & Worcester

"Professor Trachtman's book is required reading for lawyers, those who hire or work with lawyers, anyone interested in understanding the dynamics of legal negotiations or of political debate, and anyone interested in winning arguments. Its unique and practical approach strips away jargon to isolate the core elements of legal reasoning and argumentation in a way that is accessible and applicable in everyday situations. Non-lawyers will find it a useful guide to effective persuasion."

— John A. Burgess, Partner, WilmerHale

Joel P. Trachtman is Professor of International Law at The Fletcher School of Law and Diplomacy at Tufts University. An authority on international business and economic law, he has published six academic books and over 80 scholarly articles, and regularly lectures at leading universities, companies, and organizations around the world. Prior to joining the Fletcher School faculty, Trachtman practiced law with Shearman & Sterling, a Wall Street law firm, in New York and in Hong Kong.

THE TOOLS OF ARGUMENT

How the Best Lawyers Think, Argue, and Win

JOEL P. TRACHTMAN

Library of Congress Control Number: 2012923785
CreateSpace Independent Publishing Platform
North Charleston, South Carolina

ISBN: 1481246380
ISBN 13: 9781481246385

www.toolsofargument.com

To Lauren

Contents

Preface

Have you ever been in the midst of a discussion or argument regarding business, politics, ethics, sports, family responsibilities, or any other contentious topic and felt that your opponent did not have the "right" position, but had the better argument? Why is it that some people—often lawyers—can use reasoned arguments to debate with frustrating effectiveness? Perhaps you wished that you had a greater repertoire of skills both to make your points and to counter those put forth by your opponent. This book will help. Why not take advantage of the professional-grade tools of argument that have been honed through the ages in the discipline of law?

The purpose of this book is to equip law students, new lawyers, paralegals, and executives, as well as anyone else who wants to improve their skills of reasoned persuasion, with the powerful and time-tested tools of argument. Can you recall a time when you identified the loose thread or logical flaw in your opponent's argument, pointed it out, and felt a sense of vindication? At that moment, you might have exclaimed to your opponent that he or she had been "lawyered!"[1] If you liked that feeling—or if you wished you had a more persuasive way to articulate your opposing views—then you will enjoy and benefit from this book.

After practicing and teaching law for over 30 years, I have come to believe that the tools of argument are remarkably valuable. Indeed, these skills are useful to all of us who engage in small or large business dealings, legal proceedings, governmental operations, or other negotiations, and who enjoy critical thinking, persuasive presentation of ideas, and victory in arguments. After all, winning arguments is much more fun than losing them.

---

1 To use the term popularized by the character of Marshall Eriksen, a young lawyer in the situation comedy "How I Met Your Mother."

I have also come to believe that acquiring the skills and mindset to think and argue like the best lawyers is not especially difficult. The problem has been that there are few places where one can learn about these techniques in a form that abstracts the essential nuggets of wisdom from their complex historical and legal contexts. Such a presentation is my goal for this book. I've distilled a comprehensive arsenal of the types of arguments one can make in reasoned discourse, as well as the responsive counter-arguments. I can think of no better way to prepare for argument than to read this book with your own settings in mind, anticipating how you can use the tools, or how your opponent might use them, and how you can deftly respond.

Law students and prospective law students: you will find in this book a unique perspective that will enhance your understanding of legal principles and help you participate with confidence in classroom discussions and debates. Once you have a comprehensive and explicit framework of the arguments and counter-arguments, you can readily see the structure of legal discourse in briefs, cases, and classroom debate. Newly minted lawyers—and even experienced legal practitioners: I hope that you will find this book a useful refresher and checklist of the essential tools that can greatly increase your odds of winning any dispute.

If you are not a lawyer, these argumentation skills will be helpful in both non-legal settings and in any legal setting in which you might find yourself. (Indeed, these tools of argument are too valuable to be left solely in the hands of the lawyers.) Further, this book will shed light on the structure of the legal system, which is the principal structure in the U.S. and in other rule-of-law-based societies for making public policy and for assigning private responsibility, thus helping you become more engaged and knowledgeable citizens. A large proportion of the news of the day has a legal dimension, and you will undoubtedly understand more if you have a sense of the types of arguments that are used.

Of course, in some social and interpersonal settings, it will be unseemly or even dangerous to think and argue like a lawyer, as most lawyers eventually learn by painful experience. Don't try arguing to someone to whom you are romantically attracted that you have a right to their reciprocal affection, or that they bear the burden of proving that you are not attractive to them.

But it is good to know the techniques because, on balance, they will be useful to you in a variety of ways—perhaps in the context of convincing a business colleague of the right strategy, compelling a supplier to comply with its obligations, obtaining a refund for a defective product, securing insurance coverage for a needed medical treatment, or persuading the local youth soccer director to reinterpret a league rule. Consider: is there an issue of precedent? Was an agreed-upon process followed? Does the decision-maker have appropriate jurisdiction?

I believe in the importance of learning these skills because they work—they make a difference in "winning" or "losing" in the war of words. After all, these techniques of argumentation have evolved and survived over the course of many centuries because they have inherent, compelling logic. People respond to these arguments not because a speaker is overbearing, manipulative, or charismatic, but because they see the logic of the argument. Surprising as it may seem, legal logic is real logic, not separate from other types of logic. If you can bring this compelling logic to bear in legal, business, and interpersonal settings, you can be more persuasive. This book is designed to help you do just that.

I

Introduction

What is the difference between lawyers and the rest of us? There is no lawyer gene that makes some folks more argumentative, precise, or abrasive, than others. The distinctive professional characteristic of lawyers is a critical method of thinking and of argument that has a number of components. This book sets out these components, and thereby demystifies this method of thinking and argument.

This book is concerned with the techniques of argument—of persuasion—used by lawyers. The domain of these techniques is not limited to the legal system, but they were developed within the legal system, and they are used intensively within it. One of my goals is to convince you that these techniques are logical and reasonable, even when they have a result that may seem counterintuitive or unjust.

In order to see the power and utility of these techniques, it is necessary first to consider the legal system, and to understand why these techniques of thinking and argument make sense within that system. I know you want to get to the arguments, but bear with me. I will make this brief, and the material presented in this chapter will serve as important context and preparation for acquiring the skills of analysis and argument presented afterwards.

1.1 What Is Law?

There are all sorts of responses to the question "what is law?" One type of law is reasonably easy to identify. Statutes produced by legislatures are definitely laws. But there are other types of law, and the things we call "law" can have varying characteristics. Regulations issued by regulatory agencies can have the power of law, and in a common law system like the U.S., judicial decisions can make new law. Indeed, one of the things that lawyers do in response to rules asserted by opponents is to examine the rule's pedigree: where did this rule come from, what was the authority of its author, and does it have sway over this case?

A pat response to the question "what is law" is "law is what judges apply to disputes." This response may work for the incurious layman, but two groups might be left dissatisfied. First, judges cannot rely on this aphorism. They need to know how to decide what they will apply. Second, those seeking to comply with and utilize the law, including but not limited to lawyers, need to know in advance of adjudication, which rules are part of the system and which are not.

Legal philosophers and social scientists continue to struggle to define law, but a good working definition of law is the following: formal rules that carry the sanction of the state.[2] Sure, there are a lot of questions and peripheral issues. What about religious law, or the rules of EBay, or the rules of the National Basketball Association (NBA)? The answer is that it is good to distinguish between circumstances where these non-state rules carry the sanction of the state and circumstances where they do not. In some places, religious law can carry the sanction of the state, and the rules of EBay or the NBA can take advantage of the power of the state if they are incorporated in binding contracts. It is important to note, though, that the techniques of argument set forth in this book are also useful in connection with the rules of EBay, the NBA, and other non-state rule-makers.

So, we might think of law as a set of formal rules that carry the sanction of the state. Then, legal argumentation is argumentation about the

---

2 This definition does not work well in my own field of legal specialization: international law. International law is special because there is no global "state."

content and application of these rules—about when and how each of us can invoke the force of the state. As you can readily see, a lot is at stake.

1.2 Why Is Law Important?

As Tina Turner famously sang, "What's law got to do with it?" [3] Where does law fit in to our society? First, law gives us security—security that we will not be killed, hurt, robbed or otherwise treated illegally. The force of the state is deployed to restrain the force of individuals. This security allows us to carry out productive activities and to enjoy life without expending excessive resources on maintaining our security. Legal argument and analysis helps us to determine what protections are available to us.

Second, law facilitates relationships in our increasingly complex society. We live in a dense society with complicated relationships and complex production of complex goods and services. While this complexity sometimes is dispiriting, it allows us to have efficient production and to have a better material life. Law, along with other rules, helps us to manage complexity. It allows us to have more complex relationships, allowing us to be more productive.

Law, like taxes in the words of the great judge Oliver Wendell Holmes, is the price of civilization. That's why law is important to society generally, but why is it important to you?

It is important for you to know the protections available to you against harm to your person, your property, or your organization, and to be able to advocate for yourself in these regards. Law is concerned with the allocation of responsibility, and you will from time to time need to argue with others about their responsibilities, as well as about yours.

By complying with the law, you will avoid the costly application of the force of the state. By seeking to have the law apply to those with whom you disagree, you can bring to bear on them the force of the state in order

---

3 You're right. She asked, "What's love got to do with it?" If you are of the generation that grew up with Tina Turner's work, you might also recall Edwin Starr's "law, what is it good for? Absolutely nothing, say it again." Oops, right again, he was talking about war.

to cause them to behave properly and to keep their promises. Thus, the force of the state will be applied, in accordance with the law, to prevent violence, theft, fraud, and other bad and inefficient behaviors. Law is important because it establishes the terms under which the state will apply its force—by which society has agreed through the state and the law how the coercive power of the state can be used.

This is why novelist Mario Puzo has Don Corleone, The Godfather, say, "A lawyer with his briefcase can steal more than a hundred men with guns." The lawyer has in his briefcase the texts that will determine who wins and who loses. These texts—contracts, statutes, constitutions, and treaties—are not just words, but words that carry the force of the state. Therefore, the lawyer has in his briefcase, properly used, the force of the state, which in most places is stronger than a hundred men with guns.

Law is a central tool and structure of the state. In Shakespeare's Henry VI, Part 2, Dick the Butcher, in connection with plans for a revolt, says, "The first thing we do, let's kill all the lawyers." Dick sees the killing of lawyers as a way to destroy state authority (not, as is commonly thought, as a way to improve society more generally). But a more appealing method of rebellion, at least for non-lawyers, is to destroy not state authority but the lawyers' monopoly on control over state authority by learning to think and argue as they do. This book advances that cause. Legal argument is too powerful, and the force of law in society too important, to be left in the exclusive hands of lawyers.

Legal rules are formal rules, established according to constitutional procedures, that carry the force of the state. Law is important because, in a society based on the rule of law, it channels the force of the state. This is why society has developed such sophisticated techniques for arguing over the application of law.

1.3 What Is a Lawyer?

A lawyer is an expert. The expertise that the lawyer wields is twofold. First, it includes knowledge of how the legal system works—how all the written and unwritten procedural rules apply to guide the determination and application of the law. Much of this book is concerned with these procedural rules. Second, the lawyer's expertise includes substantive rules of law, like the rules protecting patented technology or forbidding the sale of cocaine.

Even though law is a field in which expert knowledge is necessary to operate at the highest level, it is open to the layperson to know some of the procedural and substantive rules—the difference between the layperson and the expert is in the scope and depth of the expert's knowledge. This book cannot address the substantive rules of law in any detail, and it cannot make you a lawyer. However, it will educate you about many of the techniques of argument and written and unwritten procedural rules—rules about the determination and application of substantive rules—that form the distinctive expertise of the lawyer.

1.4 The Work of the Lawyer

The core work of the lawyer is not to argue about what the law should be, although this sometimes is salient. Rather, the work of the lawyer is to argue about and determine what the applicable law is, what the facts are, and how the facts fit into the applicable law. These questions are complex enough, but as you will see in this book, the individual tools used in argument are not as complicated or demanding as those used in neurosurgery or rocket science. They are accessible to all. But choosing the right arrows from the lawyer's quarrelsome quiver and fitting them together elegantly to craft an overall argument that will persuade the decision-maker takes strategic thinking, and creativity.

In general terms, we can say that lawyers analyze and argue about what the rules are and how they apply to particular situations. The ways that lawyers think, argue, and eventually win arguments are relevant to dealings in business, in politics, in church, in the military, in sports, or in other institutions or relationships.

1.5 Sophistry, Rhetoric, and Winning

It's great to be persuasive when you're right. It's great to be able to resist sophistry when your opponent is wrong. It is a guilty pleasure to be persuasive when you are wrong.

Lawyers are the modern heirs of the ancient Greek sophists, the worst of whom sought to "make the weaker argument appear the stronger." The first way to define strength in this context is by how well you persuade your audience. If, however, a strong argument, as defined here, were one that convinces others of your position, then it would be impossible to make the weaker argument appear stronger. By "appearing" stronger, it would be stronger. Therefore, we need a different definition of strength than mere persuasiveness.

The true stronger argument is the argument that meets some objective test of strength, and that *should* win. But, you might ask, where does this objective test come from? Is it based on first principles, justice, or truth? Unfortunately, as culturally-biased human beings, we often disagree about first principles, justice, and truth. A more practical version of this second definition would deem stronger the argument that is more substantively appealing—the one that resounds more greatly in logic and policy. By making the weaker argument in this sense *appear* the stronger, lawyers or other sophists may subvert first principles, truth, or public policy. In order to make the weaker argument appear the stronger, they might be required to present arguments falsely. Sophistry is thus ethically unappealing.

Lawyers are trained to think in terms of legal right and legal wrong (which is one of the things that people find objectionable about them). If the law says you are responsible for a problem, then for the lawyer, that's the end of the discussion. But in a more nuanced social and relational setting, things are not always so black and white, and the legal system can ignore important shadings of right and wrong. This is not necessarily a bad thing. Sometimes decisions must be made, even if they are imperfect and even if there is a degree of right on both sides. However, it is good to remember that there is significant nuance. Sometimes it is also politic to recognize the values that motivated the losing claim and even to compromise when you would otherwise win in formal dispute settlement procedure.

Legal practice is, to a great extent, ethically ambivalent. Lawyers pledge to represent their clients zealously, and so they are charged, where their client is wrong, with trying to make the weaker argument appear the stronger. Yet, they also see themselves as officers of the court, or agents of the state, and in that role they should seek to enforce the law as intended and must act honestly.

This book is not intended to school sophists. But it does include a taxonomy of the tools of sophistry so that they can be identified and countered. While it is far beyond the ambit of this book to postulate a set of objective criteria or a set of first principles for use in judging arguments, it is within its scope to promote truth in argument. In the U.S., we like to think that our system of legal advocacy is a crucible that forges accurate application of law. In a broader social setting, you might acknowledge that competent and honest argument over the application of rules, principles, and policy will allow fair decisions to prevail.

Understanding the tools of argument will allow you to be more persuasive, to counter the arguments of opponents, and to make decisions when you are the target of persuasive arguments. The best tools of argument are also tools of thinking and will enable us to persuade the most important decision-makers—ourselves—as to what is right.

1.6 The Importance of Preparation

In legal practice, as in non-legal argumentation, preparation is everything. As you review the arguments presented in this book, you will see that by evaluating each of the components of your position, and of your opponent's, you will be able to see which arguments are available to you and which are available to your opponent. You will be able to maximize the strength of your arguments and you will be able to prepare with responses to those of your opponent. Unfortunately, greater preparation can also make the weaker argument appear the stronger.

This book provides many possible lines of argument and suggests ways to counter each argument: points and counterpoints. If you maximize your points and prepare with counterpoints by which to oppose your opponent's points, you maximize your chance of winning on points. Winners in every sport, and in every other area of competition, know that preparation maximizes the chances of success.

Good preparation consists of considering your facts and the applicable rules, and of thinking about the ways in which each argument described in this book may be applied, either to support your side, or to support that of your opponent.

1.7 The Power of Texts and the Incompleteness of Texts

Law is primarily composed of written rules. While there are important unwritten rules, and lawyers play a critical role in arguing about what those rules are, most of the work of lawyers is concerned with written rules. Written rules, produced by a government as laws, or produced by private parties as contracts or other rules, are best understood as a specification about how people will behave in the future, or at least about the consequences of certain behavior in the future.

The important point here is the temporal one. Laws (and contracts) are prepared in advance to control later behavior. Legislation is the mechanism by which societies agree in advance about what to do to prevent or affect specified behavior. This is a valuable mechanism, allowing societies to overcome cooperation problems so that they can create public goods or prevent individuals from doing harm to one another. Law is essential to our character as a social animal and to humanity's ability to improve its welfare.

All laws, and all contracts, are inevitably incomplete. They cannot be written in advance specifically to anticipate every possible circumstance. Courts or other decision-making mechanisms may be assigned the job of completing the contract or the legislation ex post. Other times there is no legal or contractual rule to apply—a gap in our structure of rules. In these cases, the law or contract cannot affect behavior or impose penalties, and any loss remains where it falls.

2

Legal Thinking

What does it mean to "think like a lawyer?" You might suppose that you have to go to law school to find out. Having been to law school, practiced law for a decade, and taught law for more than two, I believe that I can convey in this brief book the essence of thinking like a lawyer, what I like to call "the art of reasoned persuasion." Sure, there is much to learn in law school to prepare people for the legal profession, but the experience can fall short in empowering students with these critical thinking skills. Unfortunately, some law schools fail to do a good job teaching, and some law students fail to do a good job learning, how to think like a lawyer. Therefore, it is neither necessary nor sufficient to attend law school in order to acquire these essential tools.

Law school has three main educational components. First, a large part of law school in common law countries, like the U.S., is devoted to learning to argue about whether a given precedent governs a new fact situation. Second, much of the time in law school is spent learning the specifics of particular legal rules and how to look up particular legal rules. Third, a great deal of modern law school education in the U.S. is devoted to learning what the law *should* be—to normative thinking about the law.

Regarding the latter point, although law schools are improving, the techniques taught there for determining what the law should be are generally inferior to the techniques available in other disciplines, such as economics or philosophy. After all, economics offers the strongest social scientific tools of empirical evaluation of the results of legal rules, while philosophy offers the strongest analytical tools for evaluation of moral goals.

While this book conveys the essence of thinking and arguing like a lawyer, I must concede that I only learned most of what this book contains after law school. In law school, most of the tools of legal thinking and argumentation presented in this book are only addressed incidentally or indirectly. As a law professor now, I daresay that if I had read this book before law school, I would have had a more complete set of tools of legal analysis than some of my professors. I know that if I had read this book upon the beginning of my practice of law, I would have had a more complete set of tools of analysis than most of the lawyers with whom I tangled.

The skill of "thinking like a lawyer" and the tools of argument draw from a variety of law school studies and legal practice. It involves an analytical understanding of rules, evidence, and logical inferences. It is both rational and ruthless. It fixates deliberately on airtight "problem solving" for the question: how can I convince a decision-maker that I should win?

This book synthesizes what it means to think and argue like a lawyer. The skills presented include a number of identifiable and discrete components that, individually, are rather simple. When combined artfully, they allow you to construct a formidable argument. I describe these skills in clear and accessible terms, with examples. My goal is to enable you to adapt them to real life situations any time that you are arguing about principles, rules, facts, or agreements. The utility of these tools of argument is by no means limited to courtroom or other legal settings.

2.1 The Heart of Legal Thinking: Analysis and Synthesis

Here is where I reveal the main mode of thinking like a lawyer. Drum roll, please. We call it "analysis and synthesis." Lawyers break legal questions down into components, or elements, of a crime or of a claim, and then analyze each component separately. So, if the elements of the crime of murder include intent, causation, death, and lack of excuse, we analyze each of these components separately and then synthesize the analyses for a complete understanding.

It's not rocket science, folks. But it does differ from what may be the layperson's approach, which is to reach a conclusion less through the discrete analysis of components, but more holistically or impressionistically. The layperson might conclude "that's murder" or "that's theft" or "that's fraud" in the sense of common parlance, without going through the analytical steps required by law. Behavioral scientists have confirmed that human beings, more than we'd like to admit, reach conclusions first and analyze later. The legal discipline is attractive where it can slow things down and allow us to think analytically before reaching a conclusion.

This style of analysis and synthesis is also the secret of good legal writing. In the first paragraph, or section, of your argument, break the crime or claim into elements: analyze the claim. In subsequent paragraphs or chapters, examine each element separately to determine whether it is factually satisfied. Once you are finished, it is easy to "synthesize" or look at all the elements and see whether they comprise the crime or claim in question. This is the concluding paragraph or chapter. Yes, it is dry and stylistically predictable, but its beauty is in the elegance of its function. Good legal writing, like other expository writing, should be parsimonious—including precisely what is necessary to reach the conclusion, and nothing more.

All legal prohibitions or requirements, including those in a contract, take the logical form of "if-then" statements: *if x, y, and z, then a*. The initial analytical question simply asks "if what?" What is included in the "if" portion of the if-then statement? The answer is that those are the elements of the crime or claim, or of the contractual obligation. In order to determine "if what," we simply read the law or contract and determine what conditions it specifies for the relevant legal consequences. Once we know the elements, we know what goes in the "if" portion. The law specifies the consequences: the "then" portion.

This analytical method is iterative and inductive—we don't know which potential "if-then" statements to consult until we see if some of the "ifs" are satisfied. We look at those "if-then" statements that are potentially satisfied by the facts we initially identify, and then pursue an evaluation to see if they are indeed fully satisfied.

This is not different from a doctor using differential diagnosis to determine the disease that afflicts a patient. The doctor evaluates the patient's condition and narrows the "diagnosis" as she sequentially adds to the factual elements. Just as the doctor asks first, does the patient complain, second, does the patient have a fever, third, is the patient coughing, etc., until she comes up with a diagnosis, so does the lawyer use a similar technique to come up with a claim. Of course, it may be that the doctor finds no disease, or the lawyer finds no claim, because all of the elements of any known disease or claim are not satisfied.

For example, for legal responsibility for a civil (non-criminal) wrong, or "tort," there must be (i) a duty, (ii) a violation of that duty, (iii) causing (iv) harm (v) to a person owed the duty, (vi) where there is no defense such as necessity or contributory negligence. *If* each of these conditions is met, *then* there is legal liability for the tort.

Thus, legal analysis consists of (a) breaking down each legal rule into a list and (b) evaluating whether each condition is met so as to result in legal responsibility. Importantly, the elements are generally linked conjunctively; if any condition is not satisfied, legal responsibility does not result.

Analysis and synthesis answer every question regarding whether an act violates the law or is required by law. The analysis breaks the prohibition or requirement into component conditions then sequentially evaluates whether each condition is met. The synthesis merely observes whether each condition is met. It's simple.

If you can learn to do this—if you can recognize the factual parameters of each rule and then address the definitional and factual difficulties of each parameter—then you are already well on your way to thinking like a lawyer.

By the way, well-written laws and contracts make it easy to identify the component conditions of responsibility; the clearest documents will specify them explicitly. Good legal drafting consists of clarity in expression of legal obligations, and legal obligations are always formulated as "if-then" statements. Good drafting identifies the "if" conditions clearly and should specify the "then" result with precision. As you review any legal document, your main concern should be whether these "if-then" statements are clear and if they do what you need them to do.

Following is an example of good drafting following an "if-then" formulation:

> *If* Party A suffers any losses as a result of environmental contamination of Property X arising from actions of Party B, *then* Party B shall compensate Party A for the full amount of such losses.

Thus, the components of a claim for compensation under this provision are (i) losses (ii) suffered by Party A (iii) as a result of environmental contamination (iv) of Property X (v) arising from actions of Party B.

Of course, analysis is not exclusive to lawyers. In ordinary social life, we might ask whether an associate or friend has lied to us. In order to do so, we might ask ourselves, what are the components of lying? Let's say that in your community (we will stay out of the legal system for now) the consensus-based components are the following: (i) the alleged liar must speak, (ii) the speech must be false, (iii) the speaker must know that it is false, (iv) the false speech must be intended to hurt another, and (v) the false speech must actually hurt another.

We all know about difficulties with some of these components. Is a "white lie" (where no one is hurt, or where no hurt is intended) a lie? Is silence in the face of another's misapprehension of the facts a lie? The best analytical approach is to determine the elements that are required and then to determine whether each element is present. In a legal system, a legislator determines which elements are required, while a court determines whether each element is present.

2.2 The Rules of Logic and the Rules of Inference

Lawyers make formal arguments in court and elsewhere. A formal argument needs to be consistent with formal logic, and it needs to begin with a base of knowledge and build from there, using the rules of logic or the rules of inference.

So, in order to think like a lawyer, you need to know how to think. Surprising, eh? This book does not provide a deliberate introduction to formal logic, but it does point out some of the basic fallacies that can plague argument or hide the perfidy of sophists.

The rules of inference, drawn from all the sciences—all the ways in which we know things—are the customary or consensus-accepted methodological conventions that tell us whether it is permissible to draw a factual inference based on a certain quantity or quality of data. For example, statisticians and econometricians have a highly developed set of rules of inference that they use in their work. These rules can seem arbitrary, but they have been accepted by consensus as a useful basis for discourse.

We must recall that it is a social choice whether the legal process, or any other decision-making process, will simply accept these rules of inference. (The rules of logic are pretty, well, irrefutable.) For example, as you know, we have standards of proof in law for certain things; in the U.S., conviction of a crime requires proof beyond a reasonable doubt. This is a higher standard than that which we might use in our daily lives for determining whether someone is a criminal.

"Proof beyond a reasonable doubt" is a different standard from that which might be applied by a statistician to determine the likelihood of a causal relationship. Actually, statistical analysis has trouble with causal relationships, but can show interesting correlative relationships.

For example, statistical evidence can show how the likelihood of contracting lung cancer increases if one smokes. But it does not show how, or even show directly that, smoking causes cancer. Correlative relationships are "circumstantial" evidence, which we sometimes disdain, but circumstantial evidence can still be useful in reasoned arguments. You may have seen a television or film courtroom drama in which a lawyer discounts evidence that is merely "circumstantial," but the truth is that circumstantial evidence is often a good, if not irrefutable, basis for inference. Much of what we know is based on circumstantial evidence.

In fact, a statistician might ask what this "beyond a reasonable doubt" standard of proof means—how would you quantify this level of probability? The often-used convention of statistical significance states that if there is less than (choose one) a 5% or 10% possibility that an observed correlation is just random chance, it will be deemed "statistically significant." If analysis shows that the correlation is stronger than the selected level of statistical significance, does this mean that the correlation has been proven "beyond a reasonable doubt?" Aren't statisticians the consummate "reasonable people?"

Most of us would answer that we seldom can reduce evidence of a crime to statistical measurements—there are multiple pieces of evidence, each with different significance or weight. Even if we could measure the probability of crime statistically, we might feel uncomfortable doing so. But the response to this discomfort is to ask whether the discretion retained by *not* specifying a quantitative threshold is consistent with the idea of the rule of law, which is defined as the absence, or at least the minimization, of human discretion.

2.3 Thinking like a (Social) Scientist

The analysis/synthesis method outlined above is applicable to all determinations of whether there is a violation of the law, or whether there is a violation of a duty under contract or a tort, giving rise to a claim. However, it is wholly inapplicable in connection with arguments about what the law *should* be.

In fact, the greatest single revolution in legal research in the last 50 years has been the development of the field of law and economics, bringing social scientific methodologies to bear on policy questions about the law. This study asks questions about the empirical results of legal rules, as well as asking how legal rules come to be made. Law schools have increasingly recognized that the traditional disciplinary tools of law can be greatly enhanced by incorporating other social scientific disciplines when the goal is to create or evaluate public policy.

The field of law provides no insight into whether there should be a minimum wage, whether capital gains should be taxed at a lower rate, whether capital punishment is a good idea, or how long a prison sentence should be. Economists, philosophers, sociologists, and other experts have better tools to respond to these types of questions.

Nevertheless, in the U.S., and in many other countries, lawyers have a leading role in government, including in legislation and regulation. And experienced lawyers can indeed be helpful in evaluating the mechanics of a particular law. For example, they can evaluate whether courts or other decision-makers will be able to determine the different components accurately or not, or whether a rule can be applied consistently.

2.4 How Do You Know? Legal Epistemology

One of the best responses to any argument, of any kind, is simply to ask, "How do you know?" Putting your opponent to his proof can be an effective strategy. By asking, "How do you know," we are implicitly saying that it is the opponent's job to supply proof rather than our job to supply contradictory evidence. We are implicitly shifting the burden of proof.

We need to be careful what we ask because the proponent may be prepared with overwhelming evidence, but, more often than not, there may be gaps in the chain of logic or evidence. Once we find a gap, we just need to attack it until the entire argument falls. My late colleague, Keith Highet, one of the United States' greatest practicing international lawyers, referred to this as the loose thread strategy: pull on it and the fabric of your opponent's argument unravels. Highet was a bulldog who would clamp the opponent's loose thread in his teeth and pull viciously and happily.

However, the most persuasive arguments set out preemptively, or otherwise make available, how the author knows that each proposition is true. That is, the most persuasive arguments answer in advance the "how do you know" question by setting out the pedigree of each proposition. This strategy of full disclosure is less advisable where your positions are weak. But when they are strong it can "shock and awe" your opponent into submission. There is no more satisfactory feeling than to do your homework, lay out the arguments, and have your opponent concede that he cannot honestly hold back your tsunami of argument. Where your arguments are this good, it is often strategically advisable to lay them out in detail, even though doing so gives your opponent a chance to respond.

This is why lawyers love footnotes. A good footnote preempts argument by showing the support for the proposition. It allows the decisionmaker to see how well supported the argument is. Legal argument even has a particular set of rules for citation that is intended to discipline and guide the use of references. These rules require a degree of disclosure of the kind of support provided by the material cited. It establishes a set of rules of the game regarding how we assert the pedigree of our knowledge.

However, preemptive display of the basis for your arguments provides an opportunity for your opponent to scrutinize those arguments for flaws. Thus, where your opponent sees that there is no footnote or other display of the pedigree of your information, or where the footnote shows weak support, he can seek to exploit your weakness. In reasoned argument, you always have a strategic choice whether to make preemptive display of your back up in citations or not, often depending on the context and the opportunity you will have to provide the support later.

On the other hand, where your opponent fails to set out the pedigree of his propositions, or where, after examining the pedigree of his propositions for yourself, you otherwise identify a weakness, you must put him to his proof. Following Highet's strategy, you must pull on that loose thread and ask why we should believe this unsupported proposition. In a more nuanced way, you must test the quality of the pedigree of each of your opponent's essential propositions—some may purport to be well supported, but may actually be weakly supported, or even contradicted. Facts can be appreciated in different ways, and support for a proposition is often in the eye of the beholder.

There are two types of knowledge that are important in law: knowledge of facts and knowledge of law. While lawyers may be adept at proving or disproving factual statements, the more characteristic part of legal practice involves determining what the law is. Importantly, there is an iterative, interdependent, relationship between law and facts. The facts that we identify tell us what legal rules are likely to be applicable, and the legal rules tell us what facts are salient. For example, we do not know whether to examine the law of murder unless someone has died and we suspect improper causation: what is known in pre-modern detective stories as "foul play." Once we see death and improper causation, we can look at the law of murder to see whether this is a case of murder.

The crime of murder has several factual elements that must be proven in order to convict the perpetrator. If one of the factual elements cannot be proven, another legal rule might apply. For example, if there was no bad intent on the part of the person who caused the death, we might examine the crime of manslaughter, or the civil wrong ("tort") of wrongful death. If there was bad intent, but no death, we might examine attempted murder or assault as possible crimes. Again, once we know some of the facts, we know where to look. Creative lawyers are those who are able to identify elements of crimes or causes of action that may not readily fit together or be perceived as a particular crime or cause of action.

2.5 Thinking and Feeling like an Ethical Person: Procedural Justice and Substantive Justice

This is a favorite game of the law professor: to bait an unsuspecting law student into explaining how a particular legal outcome is "just." You should decline to attempt to defend that ground: the answer to the professor is that the legal outcome may well be unjust, at least in terms of substantive justice. Mere legal rules can never hope to achieve more than an approximation of substantive justice, and determining an outcome's justice is not part of the legal profession. (It is the duty of each of us as citizens, but that is not the subject of this book.)

More importantly, in a liberal (democratic, rule-of-law-based) system that accepts a variety of visions of substantive justice, the actual law that is legislated can be seen as a compromise among these varying visions. In a liberal system, we each accept that individuals may have varying visions of substantive justice, but it is still valuable to be able to make laws even though they, by necessity, fulfill some individuals' vision of substantive justice and deny others. On the other hand, in a religious law system in which the religion purports to know the details of substantive justice, all the law needs to do is to follow the religious vision and it will comport with substantive justice. Law that does not accept the possibility of diversity of values is, by definition, illiberal.

Therefore, in liberal societies, law is understood to be separate from ethics and not necessarily congruent with justice. But why is ethical argument different from legal argument? In brief, ethical argument addresses the question of what should be, or what we should do, while legal argument generally addresses a wholly different question.

Legal argument addresses the question of how we agreed earlier—in law or in contract—to address the problem that has now arisen. It addresses the question of how the law governs the matter at hand rather than how the law should have been formulated to do so. So, legal analysis is different from both public policy analysis and ethical analysis.

Some may observe that this focus on what was agreed, instead of what is right, is fundamentally unjust. However, in a liberal system, individuals have implicitly or explicitly agreed that no one has a clear and infallible vision of justice. There simply is no accepted Archimedean point from which to measure justice. Rather, individuals in a rule-of-law-based society have implicitly or explicitly agreed to accept the outcomes of the constitutional and legal process, because they have come to a belief that this system provides as well as possible a compromise among varying individual visions of justice.

This liberal perspective suggests that the procedural justice reflected in adherence to the system outweighs a particular vision of substantive justice. When U.S. Supreme Court nominees traditionally testify at their confirmation hearings that they will apply the law as written and will not engage in "judicial legislation," they are pledging allegiance to these procedural justice values and foreswearing the application of their own vision of substantive justice.

> *"Fragile as reason is and limited as law is as the expression of the institutionalized medium of reason, that's all we have standing between us and the tyranny of mere will and the cruelty of unbridled, unprincipled, undisciplined feeling."*
>
> **Justice Felix Frankfurter, 1962**

3

Arguing in a Legal System: Procedure

Consider the implications of the prior sub-section: the law itself may be inconsistent with substantive justice—it may be inconsistent with what you or I believe is right. The idea that we have a legal system rather than a system that simply says, "Do what is right in each circumstance," represents a recognition that we must compromise about what we think may be right in order to live in a society with others who have varying visions of what is right.

Therefore, argument within a legal system is different from argument outside, because the legal system is sympathetic to certain arguments that would not meet as great a welcome outside the legal system, and because it discounts other arguments that would be more appealing outside the legal system. To a great extent, the legal system itself sets the rules about what kinds of arguments will be successful within that system. The legal system is partially independent of the society in which it operates. Although a legal system is rooted in the values of its society, it also has an independent dynamic, with principles, language, and rules of its own.

Furthermore, all legal systems vary from one another. So, the French legal system and the Islamic legal system differ from the U.S. legal system, and the U.S. tax law system differs from the U.S. contract law system.

In particular, the concept of "procedure" is paramount to arguments that are founded in a legal system. In this chapter, I present fifteen tools of argument related to procedure and explain why using them can help you win.

But the critical point here is that the nature of a legal system is different from the nature of other types of social systems. This book focuses on the types of arguments that are characteristic of legal systems. And yet, because these arguments may also be understood as natural, human arguments, which respond to ordinary logic, and which are based on common realities of social structure, it is not surprising that these arguments resonate and are useful in non-legal contexts as well.

3.1 Argue About Arguing: Why Procedure Matters

You may be familiar with the story about the Vietnam War Paris peace talks in 1972-1973, in which much of the preliminary negotiations were concerned with the shape of the table around which the discussions would take place. While this particular negotiation was imbued with great symbolic value, and therefore had important outcome-determinative consequences, other procedural decisions often have direct outcome-determinative consequences—they may decide who wins and who loses. Knowing this, lawyers will argue fiercely about procedural decisions. They do so after a process of backward induction in which they determine how the procedural decision will affect their chances of winning.

For example, lawyers know that in an interstate or international case, there is a question as to what is the applicable law: the law of party A's home (say, Kansas), the law of party B's home (say, Japan), the law of the place where the transaction occurred (say, France), or something else. They also know that different courts have different approaches to determining which law to apply. Furthermore, different bodies of law may have sharply different approaches to determining responsibility. Depending on which court you are in, one law might apply as opposed to another, and the law that applies could determine who wins. The plaintiff usually gets a first shot at determining where the case will be brought, and sophisticated plaintiffs will choose the court that will apply the law that will result in their victory. The process of figuring out one's preferred court is what lawyers call "forum-shopping."

The following hypothetical decision tree shows how this process of backward induction would work. The plaintiff has a choice of suing in Kansas, Japanese, or French courts. Japanese and Kansas courts would each apply their own methods of choosing the applicable law, but we will assume that both their methods would result in the application of French law. The French court would apply a different method of choosing the applicable law, which we will assume would result in the application of Kansas law. The plaintiff believes that it has a very good chance of winning if Kansas law is applied and a very good chance of losing if French law is applied. So, once it completes this analysis, the plaintiff tries to bring the case in a French court. If the defendant sees the same picture, it fights the plaintiff's choice of a French court.

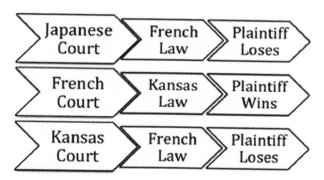

Process and substance are intertwined, and often inseparable. If your opponent has the better substantive argument, counter with procedural arguments that can change the substantive rules or that can make your opponent's argument more difficult to make.

3.2 Argue for Procedural Benefit: To Win on Substance, Maximize Your Procedural Advantage

Good lawyers, like good athletes, know that small sources of advantage are important. Each of those small sources of advantage makes our chances of winning greater, and if there are a lot of them, they make our chances of winning much greater. Such advantages on a tennis court wouldn't turn me into Novak Djokovic. But they do increase my chances of winning against my likely opponents. And certainly when the greatest players compete, each seeks every small source of advantage. Superstar lawyers are no different. You achieve superstar status by seeking every small source of advantage and assembling these multiple small advantages into dominance.

Point: You have done something wrong.

Counterpoint: The procedure that you propose to follow, or have followed, in determining that I have done something wrong is unfair or otherwise defective.

Virtually any decision can be attacked on the basis that the process by which it was made was somehow defective, including providing insufficient opportunity for a party to be heard. Conversely, lawyers know that if they want to make a decision stick—make it effective—they will need to follow an acceptable procedure. If the decision is likely to benefit you, make sure that the procedure by which it is made is good in order to safeguard the expected results.

Let's say that your colleague at work has made a decision to invest in a new piece of equipment. If you disagree, you can attack the substance of the decision. But you might begin, and you might get a more sympathetic hearing, by attacking first the process by which the decision was made. Were all the appropriate parties consulted, were the right return on investment analyses done, and so on?

For a different example, let's assume for a moment that you have committed what looks like theft: you walked into a store, put an item in your pocket, failed to pay for it, and left the store, all intentionally. What more is there to say? In a legal system, as compared to common perception and parlance, there is actually a lot more to say. For a layperson, this can be a source of puzzlement, or even anger. Sometimes we are disappointed to see a criminal "get off on a technicality."

These technicalities often reflect important social values, and so it should not come as too great a surprise that we sometimes allow the concern for the so-called "technicality" to overcome the concern for substantive justice. Many of these technicalities come under the constitutional and human rights heading of "due process." These technicalities may be hard-won protections of fundamental liberties and are established to protect the honest citizen or loyal political dissenter as much as the horrid criminal. Thus, there are circumstances where the legal system imposes limits based on systemic values that are additional to, and separate from, the substantive question of whether the crime took place.

The legal approach to "due process" is easier to see in an appealing case, such as that of a first time teenage shoplifter tortured into a confession, as opposed to the unappealing case of a vicious criminal who is caught dead to rights but is able to escape punishment because a police officer made a harmless mistake. But even the latter case might have a rationale: to deter future police mistakes and ensure greater police care in dealing with suspects. Such deterrence could be more valuable to society than even the conviction of a vicious criminal. However, even if the deterrence is not greater in value than the conviction of the criminal, the fidelity to the rule that results in the release of the criminal—the maintenance of the rule of law itself—may be more valuable than the conviction.

Back to my earlier example, if you did steal that merchandise, what can your lawyer do? She will certainly examine whether she can challenge the prosecution's depiction of the facts that are the basis for a finding that your actions satisfied the components of the crime of theft. But she will also examine other possible defenses, including those that relate to procedural issues. Does the court hearing the case have jurisdiction to do so? What precisely is the matter at issue—what factual circumstances are to be examined? What law applies to these facts? Is there anything that disables the prosecutor from continuing to prosecute the case? Can the prosecutor bear the burden of proving all of the elements of the crime, including your state of mind? Is all of the evidence admissible? If you will be convicted, is there a way to limit the penalties?

Analogous arguments may be made outside the courtroom in every-day life. Children do this all the time. If they are seeking permission from their parents for an activity, they may select the parent to ask based on expectations about that parent's relative permissiveness compared to the other. They may even ask the second parent after being turned down by the first parent. The parent may respond with the procedural rule that Dad is not permitted to contradict Mom, thus, denying the child's request. Parents also often apply a rule of res judicata, as described in section 3.14: once a decision is made, it is final.

At a more formal level, let's say that you are a student accused of pla-giarism by your teacher. You might argue that the teacher should not be the one to decide whether you plagiarized or what penalty to impose, but rather the principal or dean should do so, or a committee should do so, or an external court should do so. You might argue for a different forum in order to have a different set of substantive rules applied, or possibly to have a different definition of plagiarism. Or you might be concerned with procedural rules, such as presumptions, burden of proof, or remedies. As a teacher, I can attest that your accuser will fear that you may turn the tables on him by accusing him of dealing with you in an unfair, procedur-ally defective way.

3.3 Argue That It's None of the Tribunal's Business: There Is No Jurisdiction

Legal argument is fundamentally concerned with jurisdiction: the power and scope of application of legal rules and legal processes. A lawyer de-fending a client from charges of crime, or from claims of tort or breach of contract, might begin by challenging the power of the court, which is initially selected by the prosecutor or the plaintiff, to hear and decide the case and to impose legal consequences on the defendant.

Courts are agents of the state, authorized and empowered by the state to decide specified cases and to mete out punishment or remedies as appropriate. All courts are limited in their jurisdiction—in their power to hear and decide cases. This limitation may depend upon the kind of person being sued, or the kind of person suing, or upon the type of case involved.

Why is the defendant's lawyer interested in challenging the jurisdiction of the court? First, if the case can be thrown out of one court, it increases the litigation expenses to the plaintiff significantly—the plaintiff might simply give up. Second, the alternative court might apply a different and more favorable set of legal rules, and a skilled lawyer representing the defendant will ensure that this is so before seeking dismissal in the first court.

Any time a matter is brought by your opponent before a court or another authoritative decision-maker, it is worth asking whether or not there is any question regarding the authority of that court or decision-maker to decide the case. For example, let's say that you run a Japanese manufacturing company that makes valves for motorcycle tires. You sell some valves to a Taiwanese tire manufacturer, which inserts the valves in its tires and sells the tires around the world, including in California. A valve fails on a tire sold to a California consumer, and in the ensuing crash, his wife dies and he is severely injured. He then sues everyone. The Japanese company hasn't done any business in California. The Taiwanese company did. Assume further that California law imposes much greater responsibilities on valve manufacturers than does either Japanese or Taiwanese law.

Under U.S. constitutional due process law (the Fifth Amendment), it is not enough that the Japanese valve manufacturer's valves merely found their way to the U.S. Rather, there must be some sufficient relationship between the defendant and the state in which the court sits. Sufficiency is judged, in part, in terms of fundamental fairness: Is it fair to expect this foreign person to defend himself in U.S. courts when he has not availed himself of the benefits of doing business in the state where the court sits? Note, though, that what is really at stake is whether California law, with its higher standards of responsibility, will be applied.

Thus, interestingly, the power of a court is dependent on the relationship between the individual defendant and the state in which the court sits. The relationship must be sufficient to justify the application of authority by that court. We might ask a similar question about whether a Buddhist can be brought before an Islamic Shari'a court, or whether a university tribunal can determine whether a student can be expelled for plagiarism.

The world has many different kinds of courts and tribunals, and they often have overlapping mandates and overlapping jurisdiction over persons. So, even if there is jurisdiction over the defendant, there is also the question of whether the court that the plaintiff has selected is the best court, or is an appropriate court, to hear the case. In the 1985 Bhopal disaster, in which an Indian chemical plant owned by a subsidiary of the U.S. company Union Carbide exploded, killing and injuring many people, there was a significant question whether the case should be heard by U.S. courts or by Indian courts.

At one point in the Bhopal litigation, we had the counterintuitive phenomenon of the Indian government arguing that U.S. courts should hear the case. A government was arguing that another government's courts should settle the dispute about something that occurred within its territory. Can you imagine why?

There were several reasons, but the largest was that recoveries for personal injury or death are far greater in the U.S. tort system than in the Indian tort system: Indian plaintiffs would be better off if their claims were brought in the U.S. Other reasons included the greater ability to obtain evidence prior to trial in the U.S., the greater ease of establishing a class action among similarly affected plaintiffs, and the availability of contingency fees that allow plaintiffs to compensate lawyers from a share of the recovery rather than paying regardless of success.

In the Bhopal case, Union Carbide, as defendant, argued that U.S. courts were not the right place for the plaintiffs' lawsuits. It argued that the plaintiffs and most of the evidence were located in India, and so this case should be heard in India. In the end, the case was pursued in India.

A similar type of case arose a few years later in which Ecuadorian plaintiffs from the Lago Agrio region argued that Texaco (later acquired by Chevron, so from now on I will refer to Chevron) had so polluted their land in its oil production operations that it caused billions of dollars' worth of damage. That case was filed in a New York court in 1993, and Chevron, like Union Carbide in Bhopal, argued that the U.S. courts were the wrong place for the lawsuit. In 2001, the New York court agreed and granted Chevron's request to dismiss the U.S. lawsuit based on Chevron's promise that it would submit to the jurisdiction of Ecuadorian courts and (subject to certain U.S. law defenses) would pay any judgment.

In 2011 (yes, it took that long), the Ecuadorian court awarded the Ecuadorian plaintiffs a judgment for $18 billion. So, Chevron's argument that the New York court was the wrong forum did not work out as well as planned. Chevron responded with an argument that the Ecuadorian court's judgment was so defective that it should not be enforced anywhere Chevron had assets.

In a contractual setting, before there is a problem, it is possible to agree on where any disputes will be heard and on what law will be applied. These contractual forum selection clauses and choice of law clauses are enforceable in most industrialized countries. In a non-contractual setting, parties ordinarily do not have an opportunity to select a forum and an applicable law in advance. Similarly, outside the legal system, it is possible to agree with others in advance what kind of tribunal will decide any dispute, and what rules they will apply. You might also anticipate that when a dispute does arise, your opponent will examine that agreement, determine whether complying with it is in its best interests, and, if it is not, seek to avoid the agreed means of dispute settlement.

For a non-legal example, consider a purely intra-corporate dispute about whether to raise prices. Say that the company's finance department, led by the chief financial officer (CFO), deems it appropriate to raise prices, while the sales department objects because the sales team believes that raised prices will make it tougher to meet sales goals. Let's say that the vice-president in charge of sales refers the matter to the senior vice president (SVP) in charge of sales and marketing, who occupies a place in the corporate hierarchy above the CFO. The CFO might object, saying this is not appropriate to be decided by the SVP for sales and marketing, but should be decided by the corporate chief executive officer. If there existed rules or practices that laid out the scope of authority—the jurisdiction— of the SVP for sales and marketing, the argument might turn to an interpretation of those rules or practices.

Tribunals and other decision-makers have limited jurisdiction. It may be possible to challenge whether they can decide a case, denying your opponent an opportunity to attack you.

In addition, outside the legal system, it is possible to have disputes about whether a particular method of resolving disputes was truly agreed upon, was agreed upon for this type of dispute, or can address the rights and duties of a particular person. Where a party would expect to lose on the substance, it is advantageous for that party to seek to avoid the decision-making mechanism that would declare or confirm that loss.

Point: This tribunal will decide whether you have done something wrong.

Counterpoint: I deny the authority of this tribunal to make a determination about whether I have done something wrong.

Courts are limited not only in the persons over whom they may exercise authority but also in the types of matters over which they may do so. In Israel, for example, Jewish, Druze, Moslem, and Christian religious courts have exclusive jurisdiction over specified matters, such as marriage and divorce, within their religious communities.

U.S. federal courts have limited jurisdiction and can only hear cases that relate to issues of federal law or that involve citizens of different states. In addition, U.S. specialized bankruptcy courts have exclusive jurisdiction over bankruptcy cases. As you can imagine, there might be cases in which a variety of legal issues arise, each requiring a different court, that challenge these systems of exclusive and limited jurisdiction. Depending on how the plaintiff or prosecutor structures his claims, a different court, and a different body of law, may be required.

> **Point:** This tribunal will decide whether you have done something wrong.
>
> **Counterpoint:** This tribunal has power over me, but is not the appropriate tribunal to decide this case.

For example, the iconic U.S. constitutional case of *Marbury v. Madison* (1803), while establishing the important principle of judicial review of legislative acts to determine compliance with the U.S. Constitution, was principally concerned with the scope of the U.S. Supreme Court's authority under the Constitution. It was concerned with the question of what cases the Supreme Court has the power to hear. In *Marbury v. Madison*, the question was whether the Supreme Court had the jurisdiction to order an executive branch official to take a particular action (through a "writ of mandamus").

The Judiciary Act of 1789 had granted the Supreme Court authority to issue writs of mandamus in the relevant types of cases, but the question was whether this grant was constitutional or not—whether the legislature had the power to make that legislative grant of jurisdiction to the Supreme Court. Hence, the first question to be decided was whether the Supreme Court could engage in judicial review in order to determine whether this part of the Judiciary Act of 1789 was or was not permissible under the Constitution, which constitutes superior law. Here, and this is what *Marbury v. Madison* stands for, the answer was yes: the Supreme

Court can review federal statutes to determine whether they are consistent with the Constitution.

Indeed, the Supreme Court determined that this part of the Judiciary Act of 1789, granting a power to the Supreme Court that was not in the original grant of power contained in the Constitution, impermissibly exceeded the Constitution: the Supreme Court's jurisdictional powers remain limited to those granted in the Constitution. Yes, *Marbury v. Madison* is striking because the Supreme Court gave up a smaller power in order to establish the much larger power of judicial review.[4]

The Court utilized the interpretive principle of expressio unius (discussed in more detail in Chapter 4) to reach its conclusion about what it could do under the Constitution. Under expressio unius, a law or contract that provides a list of things is presumed to mean that list to be exclusive, excluding other similar things. Thus, the grants of jurisdiction to the Supreme Court enumerated in the Constitution are considered under expressio unius to be exclusive, even though their exclusivity is not stated explicitly. Therefore, because the original Constitution provided no power to issue writs of mandamus, the Supreme Court had none.

3.4 Argue That There Is Something Wrong with This Tribunal: Bias, Conflict of Interest, Recusal, and Voir Dire

It is much easier to justify a decision—to show its legitimacy—if the decision-maker is unbiased. We say that a decision-maker has a conflict of interest where the decision may affect the decision-maker in a personal way. Legal systems generally reject decisions that are made by decision-makers who were biased or corrupt. This impulse is so strong that in some systems, such as the U.S., even the appearance of bias is sufficient to result in a requirement that a judge recuse himself—withdraw—from hearing the case.

---

4 This is an important trick of power-seeking by constitutional courts and others. The first time you exercise a significant new power, do so in a self-abnegating way. This allows you to set a precedent in a way that will draw fewer initial objections.

An argument of bias can be made in advance of a decision: the respondent can argue that the decision-maker selected by the complainant is biased against him, and so should not be allowed to proceed. The individual decision-maker may be required, or may find it advisable, to recuse himself.

An argument of bias can also be made after a decision, although the argument seems a bit more cynical after going through the entire process, unless the evidence of bias or corruption was not available earlier. In fact, the losing party might be either formally or implicitly "estopped" (legally blocked) from claiming bias or corruption, if they go through the process knowing of the issue without raising it. On arguments of "estoppel," see the discussion in Chapter 6.

Let's continue with the saga of Chevron in Ecuador. As I mentioned above, Chevron began in the 1990s by arguing that the U.S. courts were the wrong place to hear this case about environmental harms in Lago Agrio, Ecuador. Chevron's motive was to avoid according the plaintiffs certain of the benefits of being in U.S. courts: liberal rules for gathering evidence against the defendant, contingency fees so that poor plaintiffs can afford to engage lawyers, class actions so that many plaintiffs can band together, and, most importantly, large judgments. But despite the disadvantages of litigating in Ecuador, the plaintiffs prevailed and won an $18 billion judgment. Then, Chevron in effect reversed course, arguing that Ecuador was, as it turned out, a terrible place to litigate, with corrupt and biased judges. You might say that Chevron should have been estopped from complaining about Ecuadorian justice, having argued that the U.S. case should be dismissed in favor of an Ecuadorian proceeding. Chevron might respond by saying that it could not have anticipated the corruption and bias that it now alleges.

Lawyers have a refined sense of conflict of interest, both for lawyers and for judges. Lawyers are restricted by their rules of ethics in their ability to work for different clients with adverse interests. If you find that your opponent's lawyer has a conflict of interest of this sort, you can pressure the lawyer to withdraw, hampering your opponent's case. If you feel that the judge who is about to preside over your case has a conflict of interest in this formal sense (even if there is no necessary bias), you can pressure that judge to recuse himself. Similar arguments can be made with non-judge decision-makers.

Experienced lawyers often know some of the proclivities, or ways of thinking, of particular judges and will seek to avoid judges who they think will be less sympathetic to their arguments. Often, there is little room for lawyers to affect the choice of judge. But in jury trials, lawyers have an opportunity to try to identify the proclivities or bias of prospective jurors through a process known as "voir dire." Lawyers will be allotted a certain number of challenges for no stated reason and may have additional challenges that they can use if there is evidence of possible bias.

Point: This tribunal will decide whether you have done something wrong.

Counterpoint: This tribunal is biased against me, and therefore cannot properly decide whether I have done something wrong.

Counter-counterpoint: There may be circumstances that could be understood as a conflict of interest in the abstract, but it is insulting to the tribunal to accuse it of bias, and there is no evidence of actual bias.

3.5 Argue for a Characterization of the Case That Makes Your Side More Appealing

The power to frame the question is the power to decide the case. You might worry, "Doesn't this principle give undue power to the plaintiff?" The first answer to this worry is yes, but that is the nature of complaints: the person who makes the complaint has an opportunity to frame it in the light most favorable to him. While this does give a great deal of power to the plaintiff, it is available to the defendant to reframe the case, adding other issues to consider, and claim that they constitute exceptions to the rule or defenses to claims of violation of the rule. Or, the defendant might argue that the case is not the type of case that the plaintiff framed at all but a different kind of case.

Recall that we said in Chapter 1 that all contracts and all statutes are necessarily incomplete—we can't anticipate everything. Sometimes the job of completing the contract or legislation is made especially difficult by the fact that other considerations—other contractual or social values— may conflict with the "central" rule, raising uncertainty as to how to re- solve a particular case.

For example, take a society in which abortion is thought to be legal. If opponents can seek to redefine—or to define—a fetus as a person pro- tected by the rule against murder, the result is that abortion is illegal. Note the attempt to expand the scope of the rule against murder, reducing the scope of the permissive rule allowing abortion. This type of potential chal- lenge to a settled "central" rule by proposing the application of "other" rules, or by challenging the scope of the "central" rule, is easier and more available than might commonly be thought.

This type of challenge—let's call it an "unanticipated other rule" challenge (if it were anticipated by the legislator of the central rule, that legislator might have specified the resolution of the conflict)—can be applied to arrangements or practices in everyday life.

Let's say that my wife and I have an agreed division of labor whereby she handles all of the household bills, and I handle all of the children's educational and extracurricular arrangements, such as piano lessons. Of course, even I know that I'd get into trouble if I tried to put this arrange- ment in writing, but it is a verbal agreement in the sense that we used words, which hopefully we remember, to express our agreement.

The piano teacher expects a check on the date of the first lesson of each month. I assume my wife will write it under the "she takes care of household bills" rule. She counters that this does not fall under that rule, or that it also falls under the "educational arrangements" rule, and there- fore is my responsibility. I might initially feel blindsided and feel I am being asked to do too much. But it is easy to see that there is no natural or clear solution to this problem. It is arguably both, and the outcome will depend on who controls the definition of the respective categories.

Much of legal argumentation has this dynamic. Of course, in many cases, we live with uncertainty, and we leave it to negotiation later to determine how to handle a particular case. Indeterminacy is part of social life and can never be eliminated. We might address indeterminacy, but not eliminate it, by assigning the decision to a third party, such as a court.

In fact, the framing and reframing of a dispute is an arena in which legal creativity can be most effective and most valuable. A reframing of the dispute is, quite literally, a "game-changer." Therefore, at the moment of definition of the matter in dispute, it is important to think carefully about all of the alternative ways in which a dispute might be framed. Is it a question of property rights or a question of environmental protection? Is it a question of murder or of self-defense? Is it a question of enforcement of contract or one of liability for civil wrongs?

Recall our discussion of differential diagnosis. Take all of the available facts and see with what "diseases" they are consistent. In the modern legal system, plaintiffs are often not required to choose only the "right" one. They may bring whatever case they want, and sometimes they may proceed on multiple "theories" of the case.

When people call a lawyer "creative," it is often because the lawyer has found a way to place a set of facts in a novel legal frame. These lawyers identify, or invent, a source of leverage—a claim of legal right—that others had not seen.

A dispute about flame-resistance standards for furniture illustrates my point. In 1975, California enacted a standard that requires furniture to be sufficiently flame-resistant to avoid ignition from a flame of a specified size. In order to meet this standard, each piece of furniture sold in California is treated with a substantial amount of chemical flame-retardants. Because of California's size and importance in the North American market, most furniture sold in the U.S. and Canada conforms to California's standards: most furniture manufacturers sell a uniform product throughout this territory. While the flame resistance won't prevent the furniture from burning in a fire, it will limit the ability of the furniture to initially catch fire. The fire-prevention benefits are thought to be modest. But it would be difficult to criticize framing this as a fire-prevention measure without engaging in complicated cost-benefit analysis.

In more recent years, however, it has been learned that some of the chemicals used to give the furniture its fire-resistant characteristics may cause cancer or impair brain development. Therefore, it would no longer be sensible to understand the California standard simply in terms of its fire-prevention role. We must also understand the California standard in terms of health and environmental concerns. Once these concerns were discovered, it was appropriate to re-frame the decision whether to continue to apply California's standard—broadening the considerations.

The chemical companies that supply the fire-retardant chemicals saw the possible end of a profitable business. They engaged in some creative lawyering, reframing this as a civil rights issue. How? They suggested that those at risk for fires are the poorest, and are ethnic minorities, and that a move away from fire retardants would disproportionately harm these people. Of course, an easy response is that the health effects of these chemicals also harm these people, but the health advocates would have to show that the health effects are worse than the fire effects. So, by reframing the fire-retardant chemical debate as a debate about disproportionate adverse effects on minorities, the chemical companies are able to add some strength to their side of the argument.

Point: Fire retardants are needed to prevent fires.

Counterpoint: Fire retardants cause cancer and brain damage.

Counter-counterpoint: Restrictions on the use of fire retardants will disproportionately harm minorities.

One of the most creative and valuable things a lawyer can do is to reframe the issues—to characterize a dispute as a different type of case than what was originally understood. This technique is also remarkably effective in non-legal discourse.

3.6 Argue for Application of the Rules That Will Result in Your Victory

A related question to that of the framing of a dispute is the question of the appropriate rules to apply to the dispute. The modern world is filled with rules: different rules intended to effect different kinds of policies, rules of local governments, rules of central governments, and rules of different governments, such as Massachusetts and California or Madagascar and Chile. If one set of rules does not seem to work for you, perhaps there is another set of rules that might apply and countermand the first set. Again, this is an area for creative lawyering.

We live in a kaleidoscope society with many overlapping parts and many overlapping rules. These rules may contradict one another, or one rule may simply encourage what another prohibits. These different rules may also come from different policy spheres. As a result, it is possible that a rule providing for environmental protection or remediation is inconsistent with a local property ordinance, or that a tax law providing a deduction for moneys paid in bribery encourages bribery at the same time that other laws prohibit bribery.

Point: You have violated the rules.

Counterpoint: I may have violated that set of rules, considered alone, but when you consider another applicable set of rules, my action was permitted, or even required.

It turns out that we as individuals and we as societies have many values, and there are often areas in which our values are inconsistent with one another. This is why the framing strategy discussed in the prior section is *always* available. Moreover, when we make rules, we often fail to anticipate all the ways in which the values we seek to implement could conflict with other values and all the ways in which the rules made now could conflict with other rules made earlier or later.

In addition, we live in a complex world of overlapping governments and other rule-makers. In a federal society, such as the U.S., there are 50 states, the federal government, countless municipalities, companies, religions, universities, clubs, and other organizations that make rules. Which rules apply? Which ones take precedence in the event of conflict?

Furthermore, in addition to different sources of rules due to the existence of different rule-makers, there are also different functional rules. So, it may be that a particular religious rule is inconsistent with a constitutional guarantee of civil rights or with an international law guarantee of human rights. Or it may be that a rule of freedom of commerce is inconsistent with a rule restricting movement of environmentally hazardous substances. Should religious law or civil (governmental) law govern the rights of parents to have their male or female children circumcised?

Once a particular forum has been definitively selected to decide the case, the next question is, "What rules will that forum apply?" Lawyers refer to this in the context of private law, including contracts, torts, and marriage, as the question of choice of law. In connection with areas of "public law," such as antitrust, taxation, environmental protection, securities regulation, or export controls, similar questions are referred to as questions of "prescriptive jurisdiction." The essential question is the same: which rules apply to particular persons or behavior? Sometimes the choice of the court and of the law are firmly intertwined. Thus, if a Shari'a court is hearing a marriage case between two Moslems, then it will apply Shari'a law. Sometimes the choice of court and of the law may be separated, as in a case in which a Kansas court has jurisdiction to hear the case, but determines to apply foreign law to the dispute because the dispute is most closely connected to a foreign jurisdiction.

How can, or should, a particular decision-maker, presented with a case, determine what rules to apply? How can we predict what rules will be applied? There are a number of different approaches used in different legal contexts. One, which I discuss in Chapter 4 in the context of interpretation, is the "lex specialis" principle, which holds that in the event of conflict between two rules, the more specific rule should be applied. Another common choice of law principle is to apply the law of the place that has the most significant connection with the events at issue. A third common approach is to apply the law of the place where the legal obligation arose. In law, as in life, there is often room for discretion on the part of the decision-maker, and for argument by the parties involved, as to which rules to apply.

3.7 Argue That Your Opponent Is Wrong, Too: Counterclaims

Sometimes the best defense is to go on the offensive. It's an unattractive human impulse: when someone criticizes us, we criticize him or her right back. You can imagine the family dinner:

> Johnny: "Mom, Bobby dropped my cell phone and broke the screen."
> Bobby: "He borrowed my basketball without asking."

Here, Mom is the tribunal, and she must decide whether to adjudicate these claims separately or to combine them. Indeed, Bobby might not have raised the basketball issue if Johnny had not complained about the cell phone. These claims seem best treated separately because they are apparently unrelated matters, but sometimes the claim and the counterclaim are related.

For example, in business, where a firm claims that another firm has engaged in patent infringement, the alleged infringer will often bring a counterclaim for antitrust violations—for monopolization or other restraint of trade through the patent. Or, where a business sues a consumer for payment on a loan relating to a purchase, the consumer might counterclaim for fraud or for some defect in the purchased good.

In the epic dispute between Apple and Samsung over smart phone and tablet technologies, Apple brought a claim for patent infringement, but then Samsung counterclaimed that Apple had tried to use its technologies to monopolize the market and had infringed Samsung's patents.

While it is definitely true that two wrongs do not make a right, it is possible that my obligation to compensate you for the wrong that I did you can be counterbalanced, and reduced, by your obligation to compensate me for the wrong you did me.

Point: You've wrongfully harmed me, and the damages are $100.

Counterpoint: That may be so, but you've harmed me too, and the damages are $150, so you owe me $50.

Counter-counterpoint: Let's deal with the issue I've raised first, and then you can make your claim.

3.8 Argue That It's None of the Complainant's Business: Standing

If a tree falls in the forest, and no one is around to hear, has it really fallen? Most of us would say that the event occurs independent of human observation. However, think about the possibility that a legal obligation exists, but it cannot be asserted by anyone. This is the question of standing. If a legal obligation exists but cannot be asserted by anyone, it may not have practical effect.

Or, it may be that the obligation exists and can be asserted by someone, but the people who have the right to assert it are not interested in doing so. However, in law, as in life, there are those who are interested in other people's business. They may be benevolent helpers or advocates, assisting a person in realizing his or her appropriate rights. But, they also may be seeking to assert control over a relationship to which they are not party; they may be officious intermeddlers.

Legal systems often limit the right to sue to certain people and so declare that these people have "standing." Often, but not always, standing is aligned with the existence of a protectable legal interest, or the existence of direct injury to the plaintiff. This issue is important in connection with public interest lawyering. For example, the early U.S. environmental movement depended on the expansion of standing to allow non-governmental organizations to sue on behalf of the public interest in environmental protection.

During the early days of the environmental movement in the U.S., non-governmental organizations such as the Sierra Club played a leading role in advocating for environmental protection. In 1972, the Supreme Court decided an important case regarding whether the Sierra Club had standing to bring a lawsuit to block the development of a ski area in the Mineral King Valley in California.

The Mineral King Valley is a beautiful area in the High Sierra within the Sequoia National Forest. The U.S. Forest Service was seeking to develop a ski area there and had selected the Disney Company to do so. The Sierra Club, whose members included individuals who used the Mineral King Valley for recreation, opposed the development. After failing in its attempts to convince the U.S. Forest Service to hold off on the development, the Sierra Club brought a lawsuit seeking a declaratory judgment that various aspects of the proposed development contravened federal laws and regulations governing the preservation of national parks, forests, and game refuges.

In *Sierra Club v. Morton*, the U.S. Supreme Court confirmed that under the relevant U.S. statute "a mere 'interest in a problem,' no matter how longstanding the interest and no matter how qualified the organization is in evaluating the problem, is not sufficient by itself to render the organization 'adversely affected' or 'aggrieved' within the meaning of the statute." On the other hand, the Court said that

> ...aesthetic and environmental well-being, like economic well-being, are important ingredients of the quality of life in our society, and the fact that particular environmental interests are shared by the many rather than the few does not make them less deserving of legal protection through the judicial process. But the "injury in fact" test requires more than an injury to a cognizable interest. It requires that the party seeking review be himself among the injured.

After the Supreme Court's decision, the Sierra Club took the Court's suggestion to re-file with plaintiffs who actually used the Mineral King Valley's recreational opportunities, and Disney finally gave up.

How does the question of "standing" come up in ordinary life? We all know of circumstances in which someone complains about something that does not directly affect him. Sometimes these persons perform a useful function, as when they criticize someone for littering. We may think of them as policy entrepreneurs or as decentralized agents of enforcement.

At other times, these interlopers can interfere with direct negotiations or relationships between the person causing the problem and the person experiencing the adverse effects. By eliminating the "officious intermeddler," it is easier to reach satisfactory agreement between the actual parties in interest. The acceptability of this type of private agreement depends on whether there are unrepresented interests that are being hurt, such as the interests of the broader public, or whether there are limitations on the ability of those actually hurt to act. If there are, the officious intermeddler will perform a useful function. In addition, someone who seems to have no interest that is recognized by society, and therefore no standing, may have an interest that should be recognized.

> **Point:** You've done something wrong.
>
> **Counterpoint:** Who are you to complain? It's not your concern.
>
> **Counter-counterpoint:** I am trying to represent people who are injured but are not capable of representing themselves.

3.9 Argue That the Complainant is Tainted: In Pari Delictus, Tu Quoque, Clean Hands, and Contributory Negligence

These are special types of ad hominem arguments, which I discuss further in Chapter 7: the criticized person argues that the complainant has taken action, or has a status, that disqualifies it from bringing the case or reduces the appropriate recovery. Even those who would ordinarily have standing may be precluded from bringing a lawsuit. This may arise if they played some role in causing the problem about which they are complaining or if they harmed the defendant in a similar or relevant way.

This issue comes up often outside the legal system. "Who are you to talk?" It often happens that if one person criticizes another, the target will defend by pointing out shortcomings of the critic.

This rhetorical strategy is known in Latin as *tu quoque*. Western lawyers are still enamored with Latin, often when we are expressing something that does not otherwise make sense. After all, tu quoque can be defeated by the folk wisdom that "two wrongs don't make a right." But tu quoque makes sense in some circumstances. The more relevant the shortcomings of the critic—the more similar the shortcomings of the critic's target—the stronger the counterattack, especially if the critic himself has played some role in causing the harm about which the critic has complained.

Let's focus on the *in pari delicto* principle. The rationale of this principle is to prevent one joint wrongdoer from suing another for damages that resulted from their shared wrongdoing. The idea is that courts should not be available to reallocate loss between wrongdoers.

The in pari delicto defense might be used where there are multiple parties involved in a fraud and one party tries to sue the other for the first party's losses. A classic scenario is where a publicly-owned corporation commits securities fraud by misstating its financial condition. The corporation's officers participate in the fraud, and the company's auditors go along with it. The company would like to sue its auditors for their participation in the fraud, but because the company itself is formally responsible for the fraud, it is in pari delicto with the auditors.

Here is a strange, and seemingly inappropriate, use of the in pari delicto defense. You may recall that Bernie Madoff, the financier, ran an incredible Ponzi scheme, robbing innocent investors of billions of dollars. Once the extent of the fraud was revealed, a federal agency charged with protecting securities investors (the Securities Investor Protection Corporation, or SIPC) appointed a trustee to liquidate Madoff's firm, with the goal of paying off investors as much as possible. In pursuit of this goal, one of the things the trustee does is go after other firms or persons who either intentionally or negligently contributed to the fraud.

Here is where in pari delicto comes in. Since conceptually the trustee "stands in the shoes" of Madoff's firm, it might be understood to be in pari delicto with all of these other intentional and negligent fraudsters. If this were so, these other fraudsters would have a defense against the trustee's claims. This seems like an inappropriate application of the in pari delicto principle. In a sense, this case presents a conflict between formal application of the law and doing what makes sense. The problem is that the trustee, "standing in the shoes" of a firm that committed fraud, does not really represent the firm itself, but represents the claimants against the firm, so the principle of in pari delicto is not substantively relevant, even though it may be formally relevant. I discuss the relationship between form and substance in Chapter 8.

> **Point:** You've done something wrong.
>
> **Counterpoint:** Who are you to complain—you're just as guilty.

3.10 Argue That It's Too Early: Ripeness and Exhaustion of Lesser Remedies

One way of keeping a complainant from using the forum it would prefer is to argue that the dispute is not yet ready for that forum. Here there are two lines of argument. The first argues that the dispute is not yet a real dispute: it is not ripe. Perhaps the complainant has not yet been harmed. The forum the complainant has chosen is reserved for actual disputes where harm has been experienced rather than potential disputes. An example is where a potential defendant has threatened some action that would harm the potential complainant, and the potential defendant has a legal duty not to cause this harm. If the harm has not yet been caused, and if there is not an independent prohibition or remedy for incipient harm, we would say that this dispute is not yet ripe.

In the context of challenges to administrative agency action in the U.S. government, the U.S. Supreme Court has expressed the rationale for the ripeness doctrine as follows:

> Without undertaking to survey the intricacies of the ripeness doctrine it is fair to say that its basic rationale is to prevent the courts, through avoidance of premature adjudication, from entangling themselves in abstract disagreements over administrative policies, and also to protect the agencies from judicial interference until an administrative decision has been formalized

and its effects felt in a concrete way by the challenging parties. The problem is best seen in a twofold aspect, requiring us to evaluate both the fitness of the issues for judicial decision and the hardship to the parties of withholding court consideration.[5]

In dealing with disputes, patience may be a virtue. On the other hand, for a claimant, being required to wait for a resolution can be frustrating and, at times, unfair. Ripeness doctrine reflects the zen-like idea that we should not act too early in response to a problem, but instead allow it to reach a point where intervention is more useful. It's also a practical heuristic that we should not use more confrontational or drastic methods of dispute settlement when less intense methods have not yet been tried.

Early intervention has several problems. First, the actual harm may never eventuate, and then think of all the resources wasted determining responsibility for it. Second, unless we allow it to unfold, we will not know the details of the problem and how best to address it. Third, if the dispute settlement system stays out of the fight, the parties may be able to reach a more nuanced and satisfactory resolution on their own.

Let's say that a nearby electricity generation plant is storing nuclear waste not far from your home. You might complain that this nuclear waste could escape and harm you, but is this complaint ripe? It depends on whether there is a legal rule that restricts potentially harmful situations or whether the only applicable legal rule only addresses actual harm.

In a smaller context, your neighbor might acquire a vicious dog. You might tell your neighbor of your concerns that his dog will hurt you or your family, but your neighbor might respond by saying that his dog has not hurt anyone yet. Here, the interesting question is the extent to which your neighbor has the right to expose you to potential harm. The common law rule, now modified by statute and case law in many places, was the "one-bite rule." No liability would arise even from injuries, provided that there was no prior evidence that the dog was dangerous.

---

5 *Abbott Laboratories v. Gardner,* 387 U.S. 136 (1967).

If the dispute is otherwise ripe, a defendant can also argue that another dispute settlement mechanism should be used first or that another action should be taken first. This procedurally required first step
may be as simple as a requirement to make a demand on the potential
respondent for compensation. Or it may be a requirement to enter into
negotiations in good faith. Finally, it may be a requirement to use a lower
level of dispute settlement before proceeding to the higher level. Here,
the complainant might argue that these actions would be futile to settle
the dispute, but the law around the principle of "ripeness" might require
an exercise in futility.

This question of the exhaustion of what one might call "less escalated
means of dispute settlement" often comes up in international law relating
to human rights or investment. These areas of international law often deal
with how a person is treated by his or her own government in connection
with human rights or by a foreign host government in connection with international investment. The exhaustion of less escalated means of dispute
settlement, here called the requirement of exhaustion of local remedies,
asks that the human rights claimant or investor go through the domestic
courts first to see if they can get the appropriate treatment, and only after
exhausting that avenue, move to the higher level of international dispute
settlement.

In international investment law, the traditional remedy for a foreign
investor is to seek diplomatic protection from its home state government.
However, diplomatic protection is generally unavailable until the foreign
investor exhausts local remedies. In this case, the home country may not
wish to intervene, and the host country surely does not wish the home
country to intervene until the process within the host country plays itself
out fully. In recent years, however, bilateral investment treaties and other
international investment agreements have often provided that the foreign
investor will not be required to exhaust local remedies before bringing an
international law claim. These changes seem to reflect a concern that the
requirement to exhaust local remedies may be an unnecessary impedi-
ment to a claim.

You can readily see how the exhaustion of less escalated remedies argument might be useful in non-legal discourse. When your co-worker complains to your manager regarding something you have done, your first response might be "why didn't he come to me first to discuss his concerns?" Your manager might agree that your co-worker has shown a lack of collegiality and has wasted the manager's time.

Point: You've done something that can harm me in the future.

Counterpoint: Let's examine this if and when you are harmed.

Counterpoint 2: Let's discuss this or use a less formal means of dispute settlement before we escalate it.

Counter-counterpoint: Once I am harmed, it will be too late. Compensation won't replace what I will lose, and I am not sure you will have the wherewithal to compensate me.

Counter-counterpoint 2: Less formal means will be futile, and will simply operate to make my remedy more costly, and less prompt.

3.11 Argue That It's Too Late: Statutes of Limitations, Prescription, and Repose

Somewhere between lack of ripeness and expiration of the statute of limitations, the complainant has a chance to make a claim or complaint. Statutes of limitations, and their continental European civil law analog, the doctrine of prescription, are designed to let bygones be bygones. This is the legal concept of repose—that after a substantial enough period of time, expectations are settled and it would be too much of a disturbance to revisit old issues. In addition, memories and evidence fade away, making it harder to bring and to defend a case. Now, you may be thinking, there is a counter to this: some wrongs just should never be forgotten or forgiven. For example, in the U.S., murder is often excluded from the operation of a statute of limitations. But society seems to allow some things to be forgotten, if not forgiven.

One question about the operation of a statute of limitations is when does it begin to run? Generally speaking, a statute of limitations begins to run when a cause of action arises, meaning all of the elements of that cause of action exist. In cases of tort, for example, the statute of limitations begins to run at the time of harm. However, if the harm is not apparent, the statute of limitations may begin to run only when the complainant obtains reason to know of the harm. For example, a doctor might prescribe an incorrect medicine that causes harm, but the harm might not be detected until later. The statute of limitations period would not begin to run until the harm is detected.

In 2012, a U.S. appeals court determined that a statute of limitations prevented the continuation of a lawsuit about the authenticity of a bottle of wine. William I. Koch, one of three billionaire brothers, brought the lawsuit against Christie's, the auction house. He bought a bottle of wine marked "1787 Branne-Mouton Th.J." for $100,000, in 1988. Koch alleged that he purchased the wine based on "glowing endorsements" by Christie's. He began to investigate the wine's authenticity in 1993 and received a carbon dating report in 2000 from the Woods Hole Oceanographic Institution to the effect that there was only a "4.6% probability that the wine was from the period between 1740 and 1800." The court found that the two-year statute of limitations began to run once Koch received the report in 2000, and that the lawsuit was barred by 2005, when Koch filed.

The concept of statute of limitations or repose is readily applied to interpersonal relations. If you harbor a grudge about something that occurred long ago and then bring it up, the target may rightfully object that it is too late to deal with something that occurred so far in the past. The

target may even criticize you for failing to bring it up earlier and for bringing it up now.

Point: Five years ago, you did something that harmed
me.

Counterpoint: Wow, you should have said something
then. In any event, it's too late now—I don't even
remember that.

Counter-counterpoint: I only was injured by your act
recently, and only learned about your harmful act after
the injury. Before I knew of the problem, I could not
be expected to complain, and I should not be denied
recourse now.

3.12 Argue That Your Opponent Must Prove His Case Before You Must Prove Yours: Burdens of Proof

In any argument, who will win may depend on who has the burden of
bringing forth evidence of his position (burden of production), and who
has the burden of persuading the decision-maker of the correctness of
his position (burden of proof). This is extremely important in many public policy and personal decision-making contexts. The burden of proof is
a heuristic that says we will leave things as they are unless the person
to whom the burden is allocated is able to prove that he has a right to a
different determination. The standard of proof, on the other hand, determines how good a case the person who bears the burden of proof must
make. You might say that the burden of proof is like a presumption: we
presume that things are best left as they are unless the person assigned
the burden shows us differently. Presumptions are discussed in Chapter 6.
Presumptions are a special type of allocation of the burden of proof; the

proponent of the presumed fact need present no evidence, and the opponent of the presumption must provide evidence that it is not true.

You may already be familiar with the U.S. burden and standard of proof in criminal cases. The burden is generally on the prosecutor to prove guilt and the standard is "beyond a reasonable doubt." This burden of proof is consistent with an assumption that the accused is "innocent until proven guilty." The criminal standard of proof is set at a relatively high level. In U.S. civil cases, the burden is generally on the plaintiff to prove his case by a "preponderance of the evidence."

Burdens of proof can become dramatic in health, safety, and environmental contexts. For example, gas-drilling companies might be asked to prove that fracking is safe before doing it. They might respond to their opponents that the opponents should prove it is unsafe before stopping them. In other contexts, we might ask whether the burden of proof as to safety and effectiveness of a new medicine is on the pharmaceutical company, or instead is assigned to the pharmaceutical regulator. Are new cattle feeds to be used until it is proven that they may cause harm to those who eat the meat from the cattle, or are they to be prohibited until their harmlessness is shown? (You can readily see the relationship to the question of ripeness.)

Often, the burden of proof in formal legal proceedings is determined by whether the matter at issue is part of an affirmative case brought by a plaintiff or prosecutor. If so, the burden would be on the plaintiff or prosecutor respectively. However, if the matter at issue is an element of a defense that may be brought by a defendant, the burden is on the defendant.

For example, if you want to claim that the high-priced restaurant you dined at last night gave you food poisoning, you will have to prove that they served you tainted food, and that the tainted food caused you to be sick. Until you do so, they have no obligation to prove that their food was not tainted. As we say in the criminal area, a defendant is innocent until proven guilty: the burden of proof to make the case is on the prosecutor.

Wherever possible, it will be advantageous to argue that your opponent must bear the burden of proof. Where there is no prior understanding about the allocation of the burden of proof, it is always helpful to argue for the allocation of the burden to your opponent. You might even begin an argument by making statements consistent with an assumption that the burden of proof is on your opponent. In informal discourse, you can shift the burden of proof with a simple "how do you know" in response to your opponent's assertion. A savvy opponent might respond that it is not his job to sustain a burden of proof, but yours. He can do so simply by saying, "How do you know I'm wrong?"

Burdens of proof are sometimes allocated in accordance with some sense of rightfulness. It does not seem right to ask people to be able to prove their innocence on demand. This seems to explain why in criminal law in the U.S. it is for the prosecutor to prove guilt beyond a reasonable doubt. Burdens of proof might alternatively be allocated to the person with the easiest access to the evidence. If the question relates to your own skills or characteristics, you should bear the burden of proof.

There is no natural or obvious way of allocating the burden of proof when debating whether a particular action should be taken. Those with a free market bent might tend toward putting the burden of proof on the opponents of an action, and those who are more risk averse might tend toward putting the burden on the person seeking to take potentially risky action. As you might imagine, the best allocation of the burden of proof will depend on the magnitude of the potential harms, the costs of finding out about the harms, and the magnitude of the benefits. Most of us would say that where the potential dangers of action are great, where the costs of finding out are relatively small, and the magnitude of the benefits of action are relatively small, we would put the burden of proof on the proponent of action and vice versa.

Point: I do not think you can prove that you are right.

Counterpoint: But I do not think you can prove that I am wrong. Unless you can, I can go ahead and keep doing what I am doing, because there is no prohibition of activity that is not proven wrong.

Allocation of the burden of proof may have clear substantive effects, favoring the position of one side or the other. For example, imagine yourself the parent of a child with learning disabilities. Under the U.S. Individuals with Disabilities Education Act, a child is entitled to "appropriate" education, spelled out in a special education plan prepared by the local public school district. Assume that your local school district has provided a special education plan that mainstreams your child in large classes, with what you regard as insufficient special attention. You reject that plan and place your child in a private school that you believe provides appropriate education. You send the school district the tuition bill, and it refuses to pay, saying that its plan was indeed appropriate, and that you are required to accept its plan. You believe that the school district's special education plan does not meet the standard of "appropriate" under the law.

Who decides what is appropriate? In the case I am referring to, the school district argued that it initially is responsible for deciding, and the burden of proof is on the parents to show that the special education plan is inappropriate. The parents argued that the burden of proof is on the school district to show that the plan is appropriate. Satisfying either burden of proof is tough, and substantively, if the burden of proof is on the parents, then the school district has a greater margin of error. If the burden of proof is on the parents, the school district can get away with a generally lesser standard of appropriate education. So, a lot can be at stake in the allocation of the burden of proof, even where no dispute has arisen.

Indeed, imagine a parent, with no particular expertise in education, and perhaps with limited resources with which to obtain legal representation or to hire consultants, pitted against the tax-funded resources of a school district. Should not the school district, which has the obligation to provide an appropriate special education plan, and which has great resources and expertise in education, have the burden to show that its plan is indeed appropriate? The school district might respond to the effect that it is charged with the public good and should be assumed to be acting in accordance with its mandate. It is then for the parents to show that it has somehow failed. As you can see, both sides of the argument have appealing elements.

As suggested in this example, the standard rule in most types of cases is that the complainant has the burden of proof to prove the allegations made in his complaint. The complainant must prove each element of the claim. And in the case at hand, the U.S. Supreme Court applied this "default rule" (a rule that applies broadly unless there are special circumstances) to allocate the burden of proof to the complaining parents. Justice O'Connor said that "absent some reason to believe that Congress intended otherwise," the burden of proof should be "where it usually falls, upon the party seeking relief." [6]

So, if someone complains about your behavior, you may argue that he has the burden of proving its danger or inappropriateness. If positions are reversed, and you complain about someone else's behavior, and he attempts to allocate the burden of proof to you, you may assert that his special capabilities, other circumstances, or the special risks involved in his behavior, are reasons to allocate the burden of proof to him.

Point: This looks dangerous; prove that it is safe before we move forward.

Counterpoint: It's not a problem; prove that it is unsafe before we stop.

Counter-counterpoint: Given the overall level of likelihood that this type of activity may be dangerous, and the magnitude of the harm that would occur if the danger eventuates, it is appropriate that the person proposing the action bear the prior burden of proving its safety, rather than to ask those who may be harmed to prove its danger.

---

6 *Schaffer v. Weast*, 546 U.S. 49 (2005).

3.13 Argue That Even If the Complainant Wins, He Deserves Nothing: Remedies and Enforcement

Even if you lose, don't give up. Even if you win, don't let up. There is still the question of what the complainant gets by way of remedies or enforcement. The law books are replete with stories of victorious plaintiffs who got very little for their trouble and conversely of losing defendants who were made to suffer very little by way of consequences of their actions.

There are two main questions here. First, will the tribunal or other decision-maker that you choose order the remedy that you wish? It may be that the court is not completely comfortable with the justice of your position but agrees that you should be victorious as a technical matter of law. It expresses its discomfort by ordering modest remedies. For example, it may value the level of damages that you have suffered in a way that understates them. Or it may decline to order your defendant to do what he promised to do.

Second, assuming the court orders the remedy that you wish, there is a question whether the defendant can be forced to comply. The defendant may have insufficient resources to comply, or its resources may be immune from the power of the court, perhaps located in a foreign jurisdiction.

Point: You've done something wrong, and it has caused me harm.

Counterpoint:
i.   It has not harmed you.
ii. It has not harmed you nearly as much as you say
iii. Even though it has harmed you, there is nothing that I am required to do to compensate you.
iv. While I may be required to compensate you, you have no way to force me to do so.

3.14 Argue That It's Already Been Decided: Res Judicata, Collateral Estoppel, Repose, and Double Jeopardy

If you don't like the answer you get the first time, one strategic response is to ask the question again. But this is costly in terms of social decision-making resources—in the legal system, judicial resources—and also in terms of certainty and repose. *Repose* in this context is the idea that we are better off if we can rely on decisions that have been made previously without fear that they will be changed. That is, once a decision is made, it is good for people to be able to rely on it. Get over it and move on. In addition, we want to protect potential defendants from vexatious litigation. So, we say that the plaintiff gets only "one bite of the apple." I have no idea why the saying refers to apples—perhaps it is inspired by the Adam and Eve story or perhaps by rules relating to "bobbing for apples."

Res judicata means that once a case is finally decided (after appeals are exhausted), it cannot be heard again. You had your chance and now it is definitively decided. *Collateral estoppel* means that if, on the way to a final judgment, there was a sub-issue that was definitively decided, then that sub-issue cannot be litigated again. There are many questions that must be answered when applying these doctrines. What is a final decision? Between what parties? On what issues? Precluding what? These questions represent process values that may trump substantive justice. Double jeopardy is a criminal law doctrine that prevents a defendant from being tried for the same crime twice.

Often arguments end this way: "we already decided it," "don't open it up again." Where this claim has the power to stick, its force comes from the same kinds of concerns as in the legal system: avoiding spending excessive time rehashing the arguments and repose. One question that is important is, what precisely did we decide? In addition, did we have all of the evidence or arguments before us? Was there some other defect in the process?

From a social or business standpoint, if you got it wrong the first time, you want the chance to get it right. But you don't want to be constantly re-litigating old arguments.

Point: You already had your chance to make this claim
and you lost. Now just drop it.

Counterpoint:
i.   This is a formally different claim.
ii.   There are new facts.
iii. There is a new way to "frame" the argument.

3.15 Argue That a Process Was Followed
(or Flawed): Process Values Are Real Values

At the core of the legal profession, and at the core of the distinction between lawyers and others, is concern for process values. We sometimes
refer to these process values as mere technicalities, or even worse as
loopholes, but the legal profession and a rule-of-law-based society are
committed to the principle that process values are real values and should
sometimes overcome substantive values.

It is in this context that I bring up the question, why is it that some
of the best lawyers become leading managers in industry and in government, not to mention law firms? Besides possessing knowledge of law and
being skilled with the methods of analysis and argument discussed in this
book, lawyers bring heightened sensitivity to procedural concerns that
others may lack.

So, instead of making a decision straight away, a lawyer might ask,
what process should be followed in order to make a decision; what is due
process in this context? What procedure would legitimate the decision so
that it would be respected by those who are affected?

This approach might be cumbersome and unattractive if it slows
things down too much or is too costly. But it can result in better decisions
under the right circumstances. The question really is one of choice. If the

lawyer understands that an extensive process might be unnecessarily cumbersome in particular circumstances and is able to distinguish the circumstances where more extensive processes are superior, or appropriate, the lawyer will have an advantage over someone less sensitive to process values. Good process is a central component of good management and good policy making. Perhaps this is because good process, and the kind of careful analysis that is a hallmark of legal thought, is a way to question the emotional or unconsidered impulses that can adversely influence our decision-making.

In addition, sensitivity to process values often brings greater legitimacy or "buy-in" for decisions. Constituents are more willing to accept decisions with which they do not agree if they feel that their views have been heard. Employees tend to be faithful to corporate goals if they have had a voice and have had a chance to learn the reasons for the decision.

Complainants must be sensitive to process, not only because they may lose on the process even though they deserve substantively to win, but also because sensitivity to process values brings greater legitimacy or "buy-in," increasing the sympathy of the defendant and others for the complainant's position.

Point: I am dissatisfied with this decision.

Counterpoint: I followed a legitimate process to arrive at this decision and your view was considered.

A gift for you

4

Arguing About the Meaning of Texts: Interpretation

Word, words, words—lawyers are all about words. For lawyers and non-lawyers alike, words, as relevant here, are used to communicate commitments now about how we will do things in the future. Words are used to construct categories of behavior that are prohibited, required, or permitted. Words are the building blocks used to craft the if-then statements that are at the core of commitments in contracts and laws. These commitments are at the core of civilization and of complex production and commerce. Unfortunately, our words are inherently subject to ambiguity and dispute, and these categories and commitments are characterized by a basic fluidity.

Why are words important to lawyers? Remember the Godfather and the idea that those words, contained in the texts carried in a lawyer's briefcase, have greater power than a gang of armed hoods. This is because these are not ordinary words; they carry the force of the state.

The ability to direct the force of the state is a great power indeed. This power must be controlled and applied in an orderly and legitimate way. Recall the liberal and anti-monarchist ambition stated by the early U.S. statesman John Adams in 1774, when he sought to establish: "a government of laws, and not of men." If men control the meaning of laws, however, is it not a government of men? The best response is that there is a core of meaning that men cannot change, once a commitment is made. However, there is often plenty of room for argument.

If we respect the principle of a government of laws, we must also recognize that the power to interpret is the power to rule—to apply the force of the state. Recall Alice's conversation with Humpty Dumpty.

> "When I use a word," Humpty Dumpty said in a rather scornful tone, "it means just what I choose it to mean—neither more nor less."
> "The question is," said Alice, "whether you can make words mean so many things."
> "The question is," said Humpty Dumpty, "which is to be master—that's all." [7]

To support a government of laws, the words of laws must have an appropriately stable meaning with a reliable and transparent means of identifying the meaning. This is important after legislation is made so that it is a government of laws and not of men, but it is also important when laws and contracts are written. It is useful to have clear rules about how our laws and contracts will be interpreted so that skilled draftsmen can express commitments clearly, precisely, and predictably.

Legal draftsmen, and anyone who writes or works with contracts, must be knowledgeable about the applicable rules of interpretation, so that they may anticipate how their words will be understood. For example, the interpretive rule of *effet utile* assumes that utilization of different words is intended to convey different meanings—that use of different words is not just for stylistic reasons or due to random unintentional usage variations. A draftsman aware of the effet utile rule would never use different words for the same thing just for stylistic variation or out of inattention.

---

7 Lewis Carroll, *Alice's Adventures in Wonderland* (1865).

> "What is of paramount importance is that Congress
> be able to legislate against a background of clear
> interpretative rules, so that it may know the effect of the
> language it adopts."
>
> **Justice Antonin Scalia, in Finley v.
> United States (1989)**

If it is to be a government of laws, and if laws are composed of words, then people dealing with government, including but not limited to lawyers, must be expert at dealing with words. As stated in the introduction, all verbal expression intended to govern future events is, by its nature, incomplete. It is incompletely specific because it fails to describe every future circumstance. It fails to describe every future circumstance because the possible set of future circumstances is infinite. This incompleteness is endemic to all verbal expression in law, including contracts and statutes. To the ordinary person, this is a problem; to the lawyer, it is an opportunity for advantage.

Imagine a machine into which you could place (a) a factual description of a new circumstance that has arisen, (b) a necessarily incomplete law or contract. Imagine that this machine could tell you whether or not, and how, the incomplete law or contract applies to the new circumstance. This machine is necessary in order to ensure that when a dispute arises over the applicability of a law or contract to a new circumstance, it can be resolved. Lawyers preside over this machine. We call this machine the legal system and one major component of its activity "interpretation." The legal system is a machine to complete contracts, statutes, and other laws, and to apply them to facts as they arise.

In this chapter, I will present an array of interpretive techniques. You may well ask how we should select among them—which are relevant to which interpretive situations? Even more importantly, which techniques dominate which other techniques—is there a hierarchy of interpretive techniques established in order to avoid conflicting outcomes based on different techniques? I am sorry to report that this is often the realm of sophistry. Lawyers deploy these interpretive techniques in an effort to win the argument; there are no fixed rules about which apply when, and so they all are available to any situation. Nor is there generally any formal hierarchy, [8] but where a rule of interpretation fits a particular interpretive context well, it generally will dominate.

As an advocate, the lawyer's job is to use, and argue the relevance of, the interpretive techniques that result in victory. So, skilled lawyers will act as though the interpretive technique that results in their victory is the obviously applicable one, while opposing lawyers will be able to show alternative, and seemingly equally obvious, interpretive techniques that result in *their* victory. A layperson can do the same.

"There are two opposing canons [of interpretation] on almost every point."

Karl Llewellyn, Remarks on the Theory of Appellate Decision and the Rules or Canons About How Statutes are to be Construed, 3 Vanderbilt Law Review 395, 401 (1950)

Interpretive techniques are arguments about the way that rules, whether they appear in constitutions, treaties, statutes, contracts, regulations, or judicial decisions, should be understood, and they are used strategically. For each interpretive technique, there is a response, and there is also the possibility of application of alternative interpretive techniques, all with the implication of a possible alternative substantive outcome. Furthermore, there is no reason not to deploy these interpretive

---

8 In particular circumstances, some formal hierarchy may be specified. For example, in the Vienna Convention on the Law of Treaties, reference to "ordinary meaning" comes ahead of reference to the preparatory work for the treaty.

techniques in non-legal circumstances where you are arguing about the meaning of a verbal commitment, whether written or oral.

Although there are many techniques available and no fixed hierarchy, take comfort. The choice is not completely indeterminate and random. The choice of interpretive technique is a method of argument. Some interpretive techniques will be more plausible than others in that they will carry with them greater persuasive logic—greater intuitive appeal—in particular circumstances. Some that are well known and often used can be presumed to have been taken into account by the authors of the text being interpreted. I try to present the arguments in their ordinary order of appeal, but hasten to add that the order presented is impressionistic, and not based on empirical research.

4.1 Plain Meaning and the Dictionary

Everybody likes "plain meaning" as an interpretive rule. It seems so simple. We just want to enforce the law or the contract as it is written. The problem, as I have stated above, is that the words on the paper are, by necessity, incompletely specific.

This does not mean that the words used are necessarily *insufficiently* specific—it may well be, and it often is the case, that the reasonable interpreter, applying common knowledge, finds only a single meaning. Strategic players will often argue about the plain meaning even where the meaning is sufficiently clear for disinterested persons. This is why the institution of courts initially arose—to frustrate strategic argument where the parties really did address the matter with sufficient specificity in advance. Where the words are sufficiently specific to decide the matter, there is no problem. But what do we do when plain meaning in the sense of "common knowledge" is not enough?

One answer is to refer to the dictionary. My main area of expertise is international trade law, focusing on the law of the World Trade Organization (WTO). When I first understood that WTO tribunals systematically referred to the compact edition of the Oxford English Dictionary (OED), I bought myself a copy. If we are to refer to plain meaning, and if plain meaning means dictionary meaning, and if the dictionary is the OED, then we might say that every contract, regulation, statute, and treaty incorporates by reference the meanings supplied in the OED. Thus, the OED controls the meaning of law. This would not necessarily be a bad outcome, but if it were the outcome, we would have to have a copy of the OED, and refer to it, when we write or read contracts, regulations, statutes, and treaties. People do not generally do so yet, and they may have a different meaning in mind—they likely have a different dictionary in mind. However, those negotiating WTO treaty amendments would be well advised to keep their OED handy.

"Plain meaning" has other limitations. For one, dictionaries contain alternative meanings. Beyond that, constitutions, treaties, laws, and contracts are often made in the midst of tough negotiations and are the result of struggle and compromise. As a result, their words do not often conform to the highest standards of draftsmanship. Therefore, it may be tough to infer a coherent plain meaning from the words alone.

Even dictionary meanings do not necessarily indicate or exhaust the meaning of a word in context. Indeed, the context of the contract or law may suggest a non-dictionary meaning for a word. So, dictionaries are of only limited use, and plain meaning is not necessarily simple to determine. What if the legislators or parties to the agreement use words in a special way? What if a clothing manufacturer and its customer use the word "inflammable" in their contract (erroneously) to mean that the clothing cannot burst into flames. What if it is understood that a "ton" is a metric ton? Under these circumstances, why should the parties be limited to the plain meaning, as opposed to the meaning they intended?

There is an answer to that question: we refer to plain meaning because it may be too difficult and too uncertain to charge the court or other decision-maker with determining what the parties actually intended. It may be that the plain meaning of the words is the best evidence of what the parties actually intended, and by referring to the plain meaning, we can foreclose strategic efforts to demonstrate a different intent later. In the next two sections, I discuss ways to supplement plain meaning through examination of intent and through examination of context.

Point: We should interpret this agreement in accordance with the plain meaning of the words.

Counterpoint:

i.   The dictionary contains multiple meanings. Therefore, the meaning of these words is ambiguous.
ii. We should determine the meaning of these words in context.
iii. We should determine the meaning of these words in accordance with the purpose of the text.
iv. We should determine the meaning of these words in accordance with the intent of the authors.

Counter-counterpoint: All constitutions, statutes, and contracts involve some compromise of different interests and principles. It is impossible to say what the agreement was—what the terms of the compromise were—except by looking at the text itself.

4.2 Original Intent and Evolution

In any debate about the meaning of a text—be it a contract, a statute, a constitution, or a treaty—one argument that has significant power is the argument that we should understand the text's meaning as the parties originally understood it. This approach makes a good deal of intuitive sense, especially with a recent contract: freedom of contract is generally a good idea, and if the parties had an understanding, it probably is best simply to give the contract the meaning originally understood. Reference to the original intent of the parties also makes a good deal of sense for a judge interpreting a statute or treaty; the judge should not usurp legislative power, but instead should seek to be faithful to the intent of the legislators.

For a U.S. citizen, it is impossible to begin to speak about interpretation without mentioning the debate between the originalists—those who
wish to assign to the U.S. Constitution only and precisely the meaning
intended by the founders—and those who believe that the words of the
Constitution should be interpreted by reference to current circumstances
and values. This debate is not just relevant for constitutions. Interpreters
of statutes or contracts, which are generally more recent and more malleable than constitutions, must also choose between original intent and a
more evolutionary method of interpretation.

This section will address three approaches to original intent.

1. Subjective original intent: Ask what the authors had specifically
    in mind.
2. Objective original intent: Ask what the words that the authors
    used generally meant at the time the authors used them.
3. Objective original intent with intended evolutionary change: Ask
    what the words that the authors used generally meant at the time
    the authors used them, but also assume that the authors intended
    for their words to develop new meanings as the world changed
    over time and language in common contemporaneous use adapted.

All three of these approaches are attempts at fidelity to the purpose
of the legislators or parties to a contract, and any of the three can be understood as consistent with the wishes of the authors of the text. Indeed, a
wise legislator or contracting party might in the legislation or contract tell
future interpreters how they wish their words to be interpreted. The common core value here is to do what was intended; the argument is about
how to infer intent. But there may be room to select an approach to "original intent" that focuses on the intent that is most consistent with your
preferred interpretation.

In its strongest form, originalism in the U.S. constitutional context requires that the law should be interpreted precisely as the authors—the
framers of the Constitution—subjectively intended. Given the reverence
Americans feel for our founding generation, and for the original ideas in

the Constitution, it is easy to see the attraction of subjective original intent. However, there are several problems with this type of argument.

One problem with originalism generally is that, over time, the original understanding becomes less able to address current problems. Remember that texts are always incomplete—they don't address every contingency that might occur. What's more, over time, our texts tend to become even more incomplete; the world changes in ways that are increasingly unanticipated. In the words of the political scientist Ray Vernon, all bargains obsolesce.

This challenge is not necessarily a reason for judges to step in and complete the incomplete texts, but there may be circumstances where it would make perfect sense to assign this task to judges. In U.S. constitutional or statutory debate, the question is often about what has been assigned to judges. Interestingly, those who argue for interpretation in accordance with original intent on the basis that this approach provides greater deference to the legislature are completing the text in their own way. They are constructing a rule of interpretation that is not within the text. This criticism applies to all the rules of interpretation described here, except where there is a positive law rule provided by legislators that instructs judges as to how to interpret the relevant texts. We see this in the Vienna Convention on the Law of Treaties concerning international law.

An additional problem with originalism is that there may not have been a unitary original understanding. Indeed, negotiations of contracts, statutes, constitutions, and treaties often involve some level of "agreement to disagree." The parties might have been able to agree on the words, without agreeing on how they would be applied. Contracts have at least two parties, and in a liberal society, legislation requires the votes of multiple legislators.

> *The pragmatic Chinese adage, "same bed, different dreams," is aptly applied to the making of contracts or law by multiple authors.*

This concern requires us to distinguish between subjective intent and objective intent. By objective intent, we mean we can reasonably infer intent from objective evidence. That evidence may be sought only in the text itself, in the context and purpose of the document, or, with some dangers, in the legislative history or working papers leading up to the document. The danger of legislative history or working papers is that it is not always clear what we can learn from these records.

Let me give you a telling example of this problem. Assume that in the negotiation of a contract, Party A wrote a message to Party B saying, "We must include in this contract an arrangement so that if the price of oil rises, the price required to be paid for the goods will also rise." Then, assume further that the text of the eventual contract does not include any such clause, but contains some ambiguous language to the effect that the price "will be subject to adjustment as appropriate."

The price of oil rises, and Party A claims that the price of the goods is required by the contract to be adjusted to reflect the rise in the price of oil pursuant to the quoted language. Party A argues that its message is evidence of the intent that the language stating that the price "will be subject to adjustment as appropriate" was intended to provide for price escalation in case of a rise in the price of oil. Party B responds negatively, saying, "We discussed that and did not include an oil price escalation clause in the contract, therefore you have no right to an increased price for the goods." From Party B's standpoint the quoted language contemplates negotiation of any change in prices, with each party having a right to withhold consent, rather than an automatic escalation.

In this case, the subjective intent of Party A may indeed have been to include an arrangement for automatic escalation, but it is not by any means evident that Party B agreed to that arrangement. More importantly, that specific arrangement did not become part of the text of their contract. The evidence that it was proposed in more specific terms and not included as such in the text actually undermines Party A's case.

Hundreds of books and thousands of scholarly articles have been written debating the correct method of interpretation for the U.S. Constitution. Beginning in the 1970s, a conservative legal movement sought to establish the use of "original intent" as the basis for interpretation. Because of problems in developing evidence of the original intent of the framers, and because of evidence of varying original intents, in the 1980s, this approach moved from a search for actual original intent to a search for original public meaning of the words in the text: from subjective original intent to objective original intent. The question became not what did the framers subjectively intend, but what was the objective meaning of these words when the framers used them. Perhaps the most notable proponent of an approach that focuses on the original meaning of the text, as opposed to the subjective original intent of the founders, is Justice Antonin Scalia of the U.S. Supreme Court.

Originalism of both types—subjective and objective—seeks to constrain judicial discretion, holding that the meaning of the Constitution during the founding era should control its meaning today. This effort has been viewed in political terms as supporting a particular conservative legal agenda by reducing the scope for argument that more progressive rights are protected in the U.S. Constitution. Under this type of interpretation, for example, there would be no protection for abortion rights or same-sex relations and no limits on the right to bear arms.

Interestingly, liberals have found that original intent is not just for conservatives any more. A group of scholars known as the "new textualists" argue that the original understanding of the U.S. Constitution included support for more progressive values. This development illustrates the methodological point that you must research the original intent before acquiescing in an opponent's assertion of original intent. Often, the original intent will have some ambiguity. Few of our current debates are completely new.

In the U.S. constitutional context, part of the ambiguity comes from different values included in different provisions. The original intent associated with one provision might be at odds with the original intent associated with another. We are often of different minds, depending on the context, and it is possible for our texts to exhibit this ambivalence. So, the original intent of the Commerce Clause of the U.S. Constitution may indeed envision limits on the legislative power of the U.S. federal government, but a number of other provisions of the U.S. Constitution, relating to the power to tax, the foreign affairs power, the commander-in-chief power of the President, etc., may have been intended to provide broader powers under particular circumstances.

An evolutionary approach to interpretation might be criticized by some as breaking faith with the vision of the framers of the Constitution or the authors of a contract. However, an alternative view is that the best way to honor original intent is to view the legal text as an evolving, living text, the meaning of which changes over time as society's understanding of the meaning of words changes. This latter view continues to the effect that if we did not view the text in this way the scope of coverage and the fidelity to the original intent would decline—would obsolesce—over time. Think of the U.S. Constitution's prohibition of "cruel and unusual" punishment. What was considered cruel and unusual in 1787 may be quite a bit more limited than what is considered cruel and unusual today, after the evolution of social sensibilities. So, is it faithful to the original intent simply to ignore these changes to the content of the words "cruel and unusual?"

> *In Lockett v. Ohio (1978), a plurality of the U.S. Supreme Court found that automatic imposition of the death penalty for specified grave offenses violated the constitutional prohibition on "cruel and unusual" punishment, even though it had not been viewed as cruel and unusual before. The Court referred to society's "evolving standards of decency."*

By the way, just to show how original intent can be used for alternative political purposes, let's consider the U.S. Constitution's Second Amendment right to bear arms. If the original intent is considered to protect the right to bear the arms that were available in 1787, then people would only have the right to bear muskets because that was the only type of firearm available at that time. Modern firearms, using integrated bullets instead of balls and shot, and having magazines or other multiple shot mechanisms, would be excluded from the right to bear arms. There were no assault weapons in 1787. It is tough to find a way to distinguish this limited reading of the Second Amendment from the limited reading of the prohibition of "cruel and unusual" punishment.

Let me provide an example from the area of international trade law. In the 1990s, the U.S. Congress passed legislation requiring that U.S. shrimp fishermen take special precautions to protect sea turtles from being killed in their shrimping nets. As a way to protect the continuing competitiveness of U.S. fishermen, the U.S. also legislated that shrimp could only be imported from foreign countries that had similar protections for turtles. However, the law of the WTO contained a provision outlawing quotas or prohibitions on imports.

The law of the WTO also contained an exception to its prohibition on quotas, available for measures taken to "protect exhaustible natural resources." There was evidence that when these words were first written in 1947, the authors of the predecessor treaty intended to cover only mineral resources. Animals such as sea turtles were not seen as exhaustible because they reproduced on their own. At that time, the idea of "endangered species" had not yet emerged.

So, how should a judge rule on whether this exception is available to allow the U.S. import restrictions? Subjective original intent focusing on what the 1947 authors had in mind would probably deny the exception the U.S. needed. Even objective original intent focusing on what "exhaustible natural resources" meant in 1947 would mean striking down the U.S. measure.

The WTO court opted instead for an evolutionary interpretation: the words "exhaustible natural resources" are required to be interpreted "in the light of contemporary concerns of the community of nations about the protection and conservation of the environment."[9] Indeed, the WTO court focused on the "plain meaning" of the terms "exhaustible natural resources" in a way that was inconsistent with the subjective original intent: if they are natural resources, and if they are in fact exhaustible, then

---

9 WTO Appellate Body Report, *United States – Import Prohibition of Certain Shrimp and Shrimp Products,* WT/DS58/AB/R, adopted 6 November 1998, para. 129.

the exception is available. You might call this "evolutionary plain meaning." While the plain meaning of "exhaustible natural resources" did not include living organisms in 1947, it did in the 1990s.

Point: We should interpret this contract in accordance with the original intent.

Counterpoint:
i.   Do you have evidence of your proposed original intent beyond the text of the contract itself?
ii. That may have been your original intent, but it was not mine. I have evidence that the original intent favors my position.
iii. Times have changed, and we must understand these words according to current understandings and needs. The original intent included an intent that the agreement would evolve as the meanings of words changed over time, and that tribunals charged with interpreting the agreement would use these evolved meanings. Therefore original intent and evolutionary interpretation are not necessarily inconsistent.

Counter-counterpoint: It is only the act of making this legal document according to prescribed procedures that gives it legal authority. Therefore, any interpretation that departs from the original intent lacks legal authority.

Counter-counter-counterpoint: It is equally plausible that the authors anticipated, indeed desired, that the meaning of the words that they used would evolve, as it is that they hoped that the meaning of the words would be frozen in time. If the former, it would be illegitimate to frustrate their evolutionary intent.

4.3 Context, Purpose, and Principles

It is natural to interpret words based on the context in which they are used. After all, attention to context is an important part of how we learn to use language. And it seems natural that if an agreement or treaty refers to a "ton," then in the U.S., we would think of a "short ton" of 2000 pounds, in the U.K., we might think of a long ton of 2240 pounds, and in France we might think of a metric ton of 1000 kilograms. What about a contract between a U.S. and a French entity?

One of the most attractive methods of legal interpretation is to refer to the context. However, there may be different types of context available to reference, and much will depend on the scope of the context, and the orientation of the context, that is considered. For example, if the context is a technical area where certain words have particular meanings, then an interpreter should use those particular meanings. Most would argue that the context should include the rest of the document subject to interpretation, and others would say that the context could also include other related laws or contracts. The idea is that the rest of the document, or related documents, can provide clues as to what the authors meant.

Extending beyond the plain meaning, the original intent, and the context of a statute, treaty, or contract, another approach is to argue that documents should be interpreted in light of, and consistent with, their purpose. Here, the question is what is the purpose, and how do we know the purpose of a negotiated document other than by reading the words themselves? One answer is to look at the preamble (the "whereas clauses" or "lead-in") to identify the purpose. This is why the preamble of a contract, statute, or treaty is often subject to negotiation by sophisticated parties, despite the fact that it does not itself have operative effect. They know that in a dispute, the preamble will be used as a source of context or purpose to interpret the statute or contract.

However, preambles are often somewhat "soft" and lacking in specificity, so it is possible to argue that they do not provide sufficient evidence of context or purpose. It is also possible to argue that the operative text results from compromises in the purpose of the agreement or law, so it would be inappropriate to interpret the document in light of one of these purposes alone.

A particular type of statutory or constitutional interpretation, sometimes used by European jurists, is principles-based interpretation. Here, the method is to divine the principles that are embedded in the constitution, statute, or treaty, and then interpret everything in the document with those principles in mind. This type of principles-based interpretation is useful where your position is supported by the principles that are found in the document. What if your position is not supported by these principles?

If your position is not supported by the principles found in the document, you could argue that principles-based interpretation is inappropriate. However, it might appear, shall we say, unprincipled to argue against principles-based interpretation. In that case, you could argue that the document at issue represents some compromise among different principles, or that it was manifestly not intended to carry out the referenced principle in full. If it is a compromise among different principles, or a limited expression of the referenced principle, then there can be no assurance that interpretation in accordance with the referenced principle will be accurate.

Furthermore, you might argue that the principles cannot be identified. Some contracts, statutes, and treaties will contain preambles or "whereas clauses," expressing the principles that they are intended to effectuate. However, again, one might respond that these principles are only intended to be effectuated to the extent that the operative language of the contract, statute, or treaty, actually does so. In effect, you would argue that the plain meaning trumps the principles.

Point: This contract or statute should be interpreted in such a way as to (a) effect its principles or (b) achieve its purpose.

Counterpoint: How do you know what its principles are, or what its purpose is, and how far the legislators or parties intended to effect that principle or achieve that purpose? There are few things we would wish to achieve at any cost, or without qualification.

4.4 Four Corners Versus Preparatory Materials: The Parol Evidence Rule

Lawyers are careful about what they say and what they write down during negotiations. This is because their preparatory materials, including drafts, letters, memos, etc., can be used as evidence of the meaning of the document negotiated. It is possible, in a contract or perhaps in other documents, to insert a clause (called an integration or merger clause) stating that this is not permitted—that the contract itself is the total and exclusive expression of the agreement between the parties. Often, there is some inconsistency between what is promised formally and what is said informally. Additionally, there may be some inconsistency between what is said at one time and what is said at a later time. Arguments can arise about what is the "real" deal—whether the original deal was changed, and whether it could be changed by later (or earlier) discussions.

Let's say that you are buying a car from a friend. You and she agree that the car will be sold "as is," meaning that she is not responsible for any mechanical problems it might have. Then later, but prior to the purchase, as you are test-driving it, you see that the "oil pressure" light is on. She says, "Don't worry about it." She tells you that it has been on for a while and her mechanic said that it just means that the emissions control mechanism needs to be adjusted—a minor service that can be carried out at the next oil change. After you buy the car, the engine seizes up and fails, and the car needs a new engine that will cost more than you paid for the car. The mechanic you hire tells you that the "oil pressure" light probably warned that oil was not circulating properly. You complain to your former friend—you know, the one who sold you the car—that she should be responsible for the damage caused by the failure to heed the "oil pressure" signal. She responds that she is not responsible because the car was sold "as is."

Point: The formal (or more comprehensive) arrangement overrides any prior or subsequent informal modifications.

Counterpoint: You should be responsible for what you said, even if it was not included in the formal arrangement.

Counter-counterpoint: If you meant to rely on it, you should have asked that it be included in the formal arrangement.

Counterpoint 2: The specific point made outside the comprehensive arrangement controls the more general statement in the comprehensive arrangement. (See *lex specialis* discussed in 4.10.)

The parol evidence rule, applicable in many countries, holds that if two parties make a contract, and if they demonstrate the intent that the contract is the final and complete statement of their relationship, no prior or subsequent additional communication, whether written or oral, can be used to show a modification or a different meaning of the contract. As you can see, the parol evidence rule plays a substantive role similar to a merger clause that may be included in the contract. The basic point here is that if you intend a special meaning or a special deal that does not appear in the contract itself, you are unlikely to be able to rely on it in litigation.

It is easy to be tricked, intentionally or unintentionally, by someone who seems to agree informally to a modification to the formal arrangement, while the formal agreement specifies that no informal modifications are to be effective. These informal modifications, even if in writing, won't be formally effective.

Salespeople of all types have one major goal: they want to make a sale. And so, they may sometimes make statements about their product, or about the arrangements for the sale of the product, on which they cannot deliver. Their company's legal department, however, has a different set of incentives and supplies the salespeople with a form contract that will specify that informal modifications are rejected, and the only warranties are the written ones provided within the contract. The law department's language will likely be effective to protect any overzealous salespeople, and the company, from responsibility and to deny customers the rights or protections they might have been told separately they would receive.

4.5 Extensional Pruning

> *In 1998, then-U.S. President Bill Clinton famously stated, "I did not have sexual relations with that woman," speaking of Monica Lewinsky. He seemed to be hoping that the public would assume a broad meaning of "sexual relations," while perhaps he was thinking that he was not "technically" being dishonest under a narrow meaning. Who knows? Perhaps he was trying to give himself some rhetorical space in case people found out that he had non-intercourse sex with the intern who will forever be known as "that woman."*

If you are a politician caught with what some think is a lie (with your pants down, so to speak), or a party to a contract trying to wiggle out of your obligations, you might switch to a narrow meaning of a term. This is "extensional pruning:" initial use of words with what appears to be their commonly accepted meaning but subsequent transition to a narrower definition in order to avoid obligations or refutation. In ordinary conversation, we might expect others to use words in the sense of their ordinary meaning, and the powerful ordinary meaning canon of interpretation would protect our expectations. But unless you have a way to investigate and get a definitive adjudication in a court of law or in the court of public opinion, the wiggle might succeed.

You can imagine how this could come up in a contract setting. A construction company might agree in its contract to clean up the work site at the conclusion of its construction activities, but it might later interpret this language not to include cleaning up spills or detritus that flows or otherwise finds its way off the work site. It moves from an implicit broad meaning of "work site" to a narrower one.

> **Point:** I intended a narrow meaning of the operative phrase used in my commitment to you: just the site on which I worked.
>
> **Counterpoint:** I assumed, I believe rightfully, that you intended the ordinary broader meaning of the operative phrase.

One of the essential functions of lawyers is to identify wiggle room like this in contracts, statutes, and treaties and to eliminate it. It takes a careful, imaginative, and suspicious turn of mind to do it well. While a court might police extensional pruning by insisting on the ordinary meaning, it may be costly to go to court, and there may be uncertainty as to how the court will view the language at issue. So, it is best for the person owed the obligation to preempt extensional pruning by paying close attention to the accuracy and precision of the contractual words. In negotiations, the person owing the obligation might seek to maximize the scope of potential extensional pruning.

4.6 Interpretation Versus Construction

To recap: all rules—whether they are contained in laws or in contracts—are necessarily incomplete. There are two types of incompleteness. First, there is incompleteness in the delineation of the meaning of words contained in the rules. That is the principal focus of this chapter. Uncertainty regarding interpretation is a type of incompleteness that can often be reduced by adding more specific language. Second, and the focus of this section, language we write today cannot anticipate all the things that can happen in the future. There is incompleteness in the sense that the rules do not address all of the issues that can come up in relation to the matters addressed in the law or contract in the fullness of time.

Although there is something fundamentally illegitimate about "constructing" laws or contracts so as to fill gaps, the gaps exist nevertheless. As stated above, all documents are incomplete. The ordinary default rule, and perhaps the best approach, is simply to leave the responsibility where it falls. The default rule is based on the assumption that the parties did think about the issue that has come up and decided to leave the responsibility where it falls. This is less problematic in contract interpretation than in statutory or constitutional interpretation. But you can imagine a circumstance in which it appears to be unfair to leave the responsibility where it initially falls, and this is the motivation for construction.

As you negotiate a contract with a counter-party, you should examine what the default outcomes are with respect to as many issues as you can think of. The default outcome is the outcome supplied by generally applicable law unless the contract provides otherwise. It may favor you, in which case you might decide to avoid discussing it. However, if it allocates a responsibility to you, you might want to make sure that you are adequately compensated for bearing that responsibility.

The authors of the law or contract may have lacked experience with some issues, or they may have simply neglected to address some issues that they knew of. In this case, it is possible to argue that the contract should be "completed" by "construction" of additional terms that the parties would have inserted in the rule if they had thought of them or if they had not been negligent. Once a dispute arises, the choice is whether to leave things as the terms of the rule specify, without completing the rule, or to engage in construction. Once a dispute arises, one party will win if things are left as they are, and the other party will win if the rule is supplemented by construction.

Think about a circumstance where the performance of a contract is made impossible, or its purpose is frustrated, by some supervening events. Let's say I agree to sell you my car, but it is subsequently stolen and cannot be recovered. Further, assume that our contract did not address this issue. Then, assume you sue me for the car. What should a judge do? She can say the contract does not say what to do, so my obligation to deliver the car persists, and I must pay you damages. Or she can construct an additional term as something we would have agreed to had we thought of this possibility. Actually, most countries' general law implicitly constructs an additional term by virtue of an impossibility or *force majeure* doctrine, saying under what circumstances my performance would be excused. I discuss force majeure in Chapter 8.

Point: The contract is incomplete insofar as it fails explicitly to allocate responsibility for the situation that has occurred, so we should construct an allocation of responsibility that we believe the parties would have established if they had addressed it.

Counterpoint: Nonsense—let the chips fall where they may. We should let the responsibility that has not been explicitly allocated remain where it falls without intervention. If I had been allocated an additional responsibility, I would have charged you a higher price.

4.7 Interpretation and Morality

The eminent legal philosopher Ronald Dworkin argued that laws must be interpreted in accordance with a moral perspective. Other lawyers call for a separation between positive law—law as legislated—and morality. Much of this debate can be understood as an argument about whether judges, when faced with a case, should let their decision be influenced by their own moral perspective. And, in turn, this issue can be understood as an argument about the role of judges and about the mandate accorded to judges when they are appointed; does it include instructions or permission to include morality in their interpretations or other decision-making?

As a tool of argument, one's position on the separation of law from morality would depend on the expected outcome. If I lose on the law considered alone and need the application of morality in order to win, I can argue for its important role in interpretation. Anything less, I would argue, would be immoral.

On the other hand, if the application of morality causes me to lose, I can argue that the legislature, in formulating the law, already made the social decision, including as appropriate all considerations of morality. Furthermore, I would argue, it would amount to judicial legislation, and an inappropriate application of the judge's own morality in preference to that applied by the legislature. After all, there is a moral argument for upholding the rule of law or the requirements of a contract. Procedural justice can countervail substantive justice.

Point: Our contract, or my legal obligation, should be understood to be modified so that it does not produce a morally improper outcome.

Counterpoint: The contract is the contract (or the law is the law). Who knows what morality requires, and besides, it is morally suspect to challenge the rule of law or to renege on promises. That is, when you have a legal or contractual rule, there may well be morality on both sides of the argument. Substantive justice does not necessarily exceed in value procedural justice.

From the judge's standpoint, how much to bring in of one's own moral view would depend on the mandate to the judge upon appointment: what has the judge been authorized to do? For some judges, this might not be the end of the matter because the judge might, under some circumstances, have a civil disobedience-type obligation to ignore the law and apply morality.

Remember that Socrates chose to drink hemlock rather than to follow morality in contravention of Athens' laws. As depicted in Plato's Crito dialogue, Socrates had been convicted by a jury of 500 Athenians of impiety and of corrupting the young. He was sentenced to die by drinking hemlock. His friend Crito tried to convince him to escape rather than to accept the immoral judgment of the Athenian state. (Socrates had not corrupted the young, but educated them.)

Socrates responded by pointing out that he had lived in Athens as an Athenian citizen, accepting all of the benefits of its government and laws. On this basis, he had a type of "social contract" obligation to continue to accept Athens' laws and legal judgments. He saw this as a moral obligation, even if the judgment at hand was itself immoral. Thus, for Socrates, and Plato, the law has its own morality, even when its results are immoral.

This idea is related to the point made earlier in this book that procedural justice may at times outweigh substantive justice. But it cannot be carried too far: the greater the substantive injustice, and the greater the certainty of substantive injustice, the more difficult it becomes to argue that there is an obligation to comply with an unjust law.

4.8 Effet Utile, the Presumption of Consistent Usage, and Meaningful Variation

The rule of *effet utile*, French for "useful effect," is an assumption that is made in interpretation of legal rules or contracts to the effect that the author of the legislation, contract, or treaty meant to accomplish something by the words used. It rejects an interpretation that would make a word or a provision ineffective. Without this assumption, it might be open to a party to argue that the rule as specified does not actually bind any conduct or cause any results. The effet utile rule forecloses such arguments.

Consider how the effet utile argument would be used outside a legal context. A husband and wife agree that they will share the work involved in tending their garden. A few weeks later, considering his alternative leisure time activities, the husband says, "But we do not really have a garden—we just have a back yard." This makes their agreement useless—a dead letter. The wife could respond by saying that the husband's proposed interpretation would render their agreement null—would deprive it of effet utile—and therefore, this interpretation is to be rejected. In other words, why did we bother to work through an agreement, when you (husband) are saying it has no bite? Why did I comply with my end of the bargain, while your end, it turns out, was a mirage?

Furthermore, the effet utile principle requires an assumption that each word is meaningful—that there is no unnecessary repetition or surplus. So it has unintended results if people are sloppy or like to repeat themselves. This principle was important in a case in which the WTO treaty requires that states must protect patent rights but may provide "limited exceptions" to the exclusive patent rights of the owner. The question was how large was the scope of the term "limited exceptions." The panel, led by my late colleague, the great U.S. trade lawyer Robert Hudec, held as follows:

> The word "exception" by itself connotes a limited derogation, one that does not undercut the body of rules from which it is made. When a treaty uses the term 'limited exception,' the word 'limited' must be given a meaning separate from the limitation implicit in the word 'exception' itself. The term 'limited exception' must therefore be read to connote a narrow exception—one which makes only a small diminution of the rights in question.[10]

---

10 WTO Panel Report, Canada—Patent Protection of Pharmaceutical Products (2000).

The phrase "limited exception," with the assumption that exceptions are always, well, "exceptional" and therefore narrow, must have a narrower meaning than the word "exception" standing alone. Otherwise, the word "limited" would have no effet utile.

A corollary of effet utile is the presumption of consistent usage: where a text uses the same term in multiple places, it is assumed to mean the same thing. Now, I can give you some examples where assuming a term to mean the same thing in different contexts within the same text would lead to absurd results. So, the presumption of consistent usage should yield to a context-based interpretation as well as to the principle described below: the avoidance of absurdity. Conversely, the presumption of meaningful variation holds that when different terms are used within a single text, they are presumed to mean different things.

You may be thinking that all these rules of interpretation put a great burden of precision on the draftsman. And I am here to tell you that draftsmen often fail to carry this burden. So, in real world terms, the overly rigorous application of effet utile and its corollaries may be counterproductive, frustrating the ability of draftsmen of agreements and laws to achieve the purposes they strive, albeit imperfectly, to achieve.

Point: Each word must be ascribed utility and meaning, the use of different words must mean different things, and the use of the same words must mean the same thing.

Counterpoint: Agreements and laws are sometimes completed after little sleep and in a hurry, and draftsmen are not perfect. We should be cautious in setting a standard so high that it will frustrate the imperfectly expressed intent of the parties.

4.9 Avoid Absurdity

Contracts, and statutes, should not be construed in such a way as to make them absurd. This is known as the "British Rule" of interpretation. In modern society, however, one person's absurdity may be another's desired outcome, so we cannot put too much faith in a sense of the absurd. The impulse to avoid absurdity is another way of ensuring that the rule that has been agreed or legislated has some sensible effect, preferably the one intended.

There are two types of absurdity. One is where the text itself seems to be absurd in the sense that a word or clause is patently wrong or in the sense that it seems to be operating at cross-purposes. The second is where the result seems strange. The cross-purposes and the strange result may be matters of degree or may exist only in the eye of the beholder. Therefore, it may be tough to criticize an outcome as absurd. Even where a word or clause is patently wrong, as in a clear typographical error, it is not impossible to argue that the contract or law should be enforced as written or not enforced at all. And sometimes a counter-party who is unhappy with the arrangement may be uncooperative in correcting the error. Better to proofread.

> "The Bolognian law . . . which enacted 'that whoever drew blood in the streets should be punished with the utmost severity,' was held after long debate not to extend to the surgeon, who opened the vein of a person who fell down in the street with a fit."
>
> **William Blackstone, Commentaries on the Laws of England (1765-1769)**

Your first response to this quote from Blackstone (perhaps after you feel gratitude to have modern medical care available to you) should be, "They needed a long debate for that?" Indeed, the long debate was probably occasioned by the concern of textualists that the law be applied as written, without modification based on the apparent purpose of the law or the absurdity of punishing a surgeon trying (however ignorantly) to save someone's life. In the end, substance and the avoidance of absurdity won out, but perhaps you can imagine a circumstance where substance and the avoidance of absurdity might be less appealing, and a tribunal would decide to let textualism reign, despite its seeming over-inclusiveness.

Point: The application of this contractual provision or law to the case at hand would be absurd—we cannot assume that the authors intended an absurd outcome.

Counterpoint: We should apply the text as written, and leave it to the authors to amend their text if the language is defective or if the application to a particular type of case is undesirable.

Counter-counterpoint: The authors assumed that tribunals and others working with these rules would avoid absurd results.

Counter-counter-counterpoint: How do you know what they thought was absurd, except by examining the text?

4.10 Lex Specialis: The Assumption That the Specific Trumps the General

Industrialized countries are dense with rules. Rules can have overlapping coverage and may conflict. Even within contracts, the outcome of a dispute may vary depending on which part of the contract is applicable. One tool of interpretation used to deal with this problem of conflict is *lex specialis* (*lex specialis derogat legi generali*): when faced with a conflict between rules, choose the one that applies more specifically to the facts. This approach assumes, perhaps heroically, that we can distinguish between greater and lesser specificity. The assumption behind lex specialis is that the more specific provision was more tightly reasoned and more tightly tailored to the subject, compared to the less specific provision. This is not necessarily so, but who am I to argue with the great utilitarian philosopher Jeremy Bentham? He said, "the particular provision is established upon a nearer and more exact view of the subject than the general, of which it may be regarded as a correction." [11]

An important example of the lex specialis argument came up in the World Court's Advisory Opinion on the Legality of the Threat or Use of Nuclear Weapons. Essentially, the anti-nuclear weapon side argued that the use of nuclear weapons would violate the human right to life protected in Article 6 of the International Covenant on Civil and Political Rights (ICCPR). This argument was a creative extension of the right to life beyond what the framers of the ICCPR had probably anticipated.

In the Nuclear Weapons case, there was a special type of contradiction between the laws regulating armed conflict (international humanitarian law), which did not prohibit the use of nuclear weapons, and the general prohibition against arbitrary deprivation of life under the ICCPR. Here, it is not so easy to say that the former is specific, largely because the *permission* for use of nuclear weapons under international humanitarian law was never legislated—there was no *conscious* specific law that was affirmatively created. However, the World Court did find that the rule of

---

11 Jeremy Bentham, *A Complete Code of Laws, 3, The Works of Jeremy Bentham* (1843).

permissibility under the laws of war was more specific than the prohibition against arbitrary deprivation of life and so dominated on the grounds
of lex specialis.

Note, interestingly, that this is a special type of "conflict" insofar as the
laws regulating armed conflict do not *require* the use of nuclear weapons,
and so it would have been possible for a state to comply with both legal
rules simply by not using nuclear weapons. Nevertheless, the lex specialis
won out in the World Court. Here is what the World Court said:

> In principle, the right not arbitrarily to be deprived of
> one's life applies also in hostilities. The test of what is an
> arbitrary deprivation of life, however, then falls to be de-
> termined by the applicable lex specialis, namely, the law
> applicable in armed conflict, which is designed to regu-
> late the conduct of hostilities. Thus whether a particular
> loss of life, through the use of a certain weapon in war-
> fare, is to be considered an arbitrary deprivation of life
> contrary to Article 6 of the [ICCPR], can only be decided
> by reference to the law applicable in armed conflict and
> not deduced from the terms of the [ICCPR] itself.[12]

The lex specialis rule of interpretation also applies in private contracts, where the agreement has two contradictory rules. In both laws
and contracts, so long as the draftsman is aware of lex specialis, it is appropriate to apply it. Yet, the careful draftsman will not rely on this principle to establish hierarchies within a law or a contract, so we may even
draw a contrary inference: that the draftsman was unaware of any conflict
between two rules and expressed no intent as to which—the more specific or the more general—is to dominate. Where there is evidence that
the draftsman or parties had a different hierarchy of norms—placing the
more general above the more specific—there is no particular reason to
follow lex specialis.

---

12 Advisory Opinion on the Legality of the Threat or Use of Nuclear Weapons (1996).

Point: We have two conflicting principles, so the more specialized one should take priority over the more general one.

Counterpoint:
i. How can you determine which is the more specialized principle?
ii. The more general principle should supervene the more specific one, because it is a broader principle.

Counter-counterpoint: The more specific principle obviously reflects the more specific intent of the legislators or of the parties to the contract.

Counter-counterpoint: Lex specialis seems to be a way of inferring the intent of the parties as to which norm should trump the other. If there is better evidence of intent, we should use it.

4.11 Expressio Unius (and Ejusdem Generis): Examples Matter

Expressio unius is another canon of interpretation. The full expression is "*expressio unius est exclusio alterius*," meaning that the express mention of one thing excludes all others. It recognizes that positive statements can serve as the basis for negative inferences, and it works like this. If we list a group of items that are covered by our agreement, and there is another type of item like those listed that is not on the list, then we must have intended to exclude the additional type of item. That is, listing some things of a particular type and omitting other things of that type is presumed to be intentional. As you can see, it is motivated to some extent by the same idea as the effet utile principle—we assume that draftsmen know what they're doing.

You can no doubt imagine making just the opposite argument. For example, we listed sailboats, motorboats, rowboats, and canoes—of course, we meant to include kayaks—for almost all purposes, there's no salient difference. Even more surprising, if a general category is expressed, and examples follow, the examples may have the effect of *limiting* the scope of the general category. This is the interpretive principle of *ejusdem generis*, and it is understood as a more refined version of expressio unius.

Furthermore, the expressio unius principle is highly dependent on context. It may indeed be the case that the thing or things mentioned are simply the most common or well-known items, but we implicitly intended for other items to be covered as well. This situation is more likely to occur in an informal circumstance as opposed to a formal context involving a contract or a statute.

Expressio unius is a rule of interpretation that assumes knowledge and intent on the part of the draftsman. It assumes that the draftsman knew about kayaks and must have intentionally omitted them from the list. In the real world, including the real legal world, draftsmen often fail to meet this standard. The result is that expressio unius may be quite inconsistent with the draftsman's intent.

Children have used the expressio unius rule to their advantage from time immemorial. If their mother tells them not to watch television or play computer games, they will play the games on their cell phone or on another portable gaming device. The parent will remonstrate with the child to the effect that "I meant all electronic entertainment," while the child will respond that the parent did not mention cell phones.

There are many examples of legal disputes in which the expressio unius card was played. In constitutional adjudication in the U.S., and also in many types of statutory interpretation, questions often come up regarding the powers of branches of government or of administrative agencies. A leading case mentioned earlier, *Marbury v. Madison*, is an example. There, as you may recall, the question was the scope of power of review accorded by the U.S. Constitution to federal courts. Because certain types of cases were mentioned in the Constitution as within the federal judicial power, but the particular type at issue was not, the Supreme Court found that the judicial power did not include the unlisted type of issue.

One anticipatory response to an expressio unius ploy is to specify a catchall category. Parents learn quickly to formulate their instructions this way: "Do not use the television, computer games, *or any other electronics.*" Contracts and statutes may use the same device. Then the argument becomes whether the specific items mentioned may be used to interpret—to restrict the scope of—the catchall category under ejusdem generis. Lawyers avoid this by explicit statements, such as "including, without limitation, television and computer games."

Suppose that the child, under the restriction including the catchall, begins to engage in text messaging conversations with friends. The parent might argue that it is a form of electronic entertainment and therefore a violation of the prohibition. The child might argue that texting is communication, not entertainment, and the child's argument might be bolstered by the fact that the specifically listed items—television and computer games—are not the same type of communication. The ejusdem generis principle supports the child's argument: the specification of examples tends to restrict the general category of which they are examples. Therefore, from this standpoint, the parent could establish the broader prohibition by simply prohibiting the general category of electronics, without listing examples. Alternatively, the parent could use the lawyer's phrase "including, without limitation" in his instructions to his child. It takes a lot of restraint not to do so.

Two abbreviations are relevant here: i.e. and e.g. "I.e." is an abbreviation for the Latin words "id est," which mean "that is." "E.g." is an abbreviation for the Latin words "exempli gratia," which mean "for the sake of example." Their effects differ dramatically. "I.e." indicates that what follows is a paraphrase of the prior clause, while "e.g." means what follows are examples of a broader covered category. "E.g." implies an incomplete list—that other things in the category are intended. So, "i.e." allows an expressio unius argument, while "e.g." blocks the expressio unius argument, as a somewhat less explicit alternative to saying "including, without limitation."

Point: We listed the types of things included, and the thing at issue is not on the list—therefore, it is not included and can be presumed to be intentionally excluded.

Counterpoint: The thing at issue is of a similar type to those on the list, raising the same concerns. The listing should be understood as a specification of examples, and the interpreter should construe the list to include other things of similar type.

Counter-counterpoint: The draftsman of the text knew about those other things, and so it makes sense to assume that they were intentionally excluded.

4.12 Clear Statement Rules, Interpretation Against the Draftsman, and the Rule of Lenity

Sometimes it makes sense to put the burden of clear speaking on the rule-maker or, in contractual settings, on the person who takes responsibility for writing down the rule. This is known as a clear statement rule.

In criminal cases, it may be unfair, and a violation of rights to due process of law, to prosecute someone criminally under a vague rule. If it is vague, it may be difficult to determine how to comply, and the rule may be subject to inconsistent interpretation and application. The rule of lenity says that vague criminal statutes should be construed in favor of the defendant.

But sometimes an interpretive rule, such as a clear statement rule, is intended to put the burden of actually deciding, and of paying the political or public relations costs of deciding, on the legislature instead of on the tribunal charged with applying the rule. If the statement is not clear, and the tribunal applies it in an unpopular way, then the tribunal bears the political costs, while the legislature avoids the political costs. So, clear statement rules are a way for courts to avoid responsibility and put the onus of decision on the legislature.

Clear statement rules are also a way for courts to defend certain principles, again by forcing the legislature to bear the political costs of contradicting the principle clearly rather than in an obtuse way. Clear statement rules provide that the legislature may only contradict the protected principle if it does so clearly. Without a clear statement rule, the legislature can contradict the principle in an obtuse way, and blame the court for doing the damage to the principle rather than bearing the blame themselves.

Clear statement rules have been used to great effect in the context of the power of Congress to legislate under the U.S. Constitution. In this context, clear statement rules are applied in cases in which the federal government has a certain ultimate power, so there is no direct constitutional restriction on Congress' exercise of the power. However, the exercise of the power is seen as threatening to a constitutional or other *principle or value* (as opposed to a firm rule), and so the U.S. Supreme Court has developed these clear statement rules to require Congress to act affirmatively and clearly if it wishes to make incursions on these principles. Yes, it is a form of judicial activism, and you might well ask where the courts get the power to divine principles and establish special protections for them.

For example, one prominent clear statement rule established by the U.S. Supreme Court holds that absent a clear statement to the contrary, statutes are not to be interpreted to intrude upon the sovereignty of the states by regulating state activities.[13]

---

13 *Gregory v. Ashcroft*, 501 U.S. 452, 460 (1991).

Point: (in the context of U.S. constitutional law): Where a statute would operate to reduce the achievement of a constitutional "value," it shall be interpreted as doing so only where the legislature has done so in a clear statement. This is to ensure that the expected political accountability of legislators for impairing this constitutional value can be effective.

Counterpoint:
i.   It seems an inappropriate exercise of judicial power to develop these prioritized "values" that do not appear in the text of the Constitution.
ii. It is difficult, and seems highly subjective, to determine which statements are clear and which are not.

Counter-counterpoint: (as to counterpoint (i)): Assuming that legislatures are well aware of the judicially-applied clear statement rule, the legislature is capable of stating its intent clearly, so there is no judicial usurpation.

Counter-counter-counterpoint: But this puts inappropriate pressure on the legislature to state certain things clearly, and even to bear certain political costs, in a way that is not prescribed in the Constitution.

A related principle of interpretation comes up in contracts, where it is sometimes argued that if there is an ambiguity in the contract, it should be resolved in a way that is adverse to the party responsible for the drafting of the contract.

For example, there is a case in which Pacific Gas and Electric (PG&E) experienced losses due to action by a contractor that damaged one of PG&E's electric turbines.[14] PG&E had used a form contract to procure

---

14 *Pacific Gas & Electric Co. v. G.W. Thomas Drayage & Rigging Co,* 62 Cal. Rptr. 203 (Cal. Ct. App. 1967).

the contractor's services. In the contract, there was a clause providing an "indemnity" to PG&E for all "loss, damage, expense and liability resulting from injury to or death of person or injury to property, arising out of or in any way connected with the performance of this contract."

The question for the court was whether an "indemnity" was intended to protect PG&E from losses it incurred directly or only for losses it incurred by virtue of claims by *third persons*. The court found that under California law, an "indemnity is a contract by which one engages to save another from a legal consequence of the conduct of one of the parties, or of some other person." Furthermore, "a 'legal consequence' is one imposed by law."

Here, PG&E had direct losses, and its losses were not understood as imposed by law. So, these losses did not seem to qualify for an "indemnity." Even so, the court found that there was ambiguity because of the clear text of the indemnity relating to "loss ... resulting from injury to property." However, it determined to resolve the ambiguity against the draftsman of the form contract, PG&E, and therefore found that the contractor was not required to pay PG&E under the indemnity clause.

Point: Any ambiguity in this agreement should be resolved against the position of the person responsible for drafting it.

Counterpoint: It takes two to tango: this document was accepted by both of us, so we are both responsible for it. It would be strange to punish those who take on the responsibility of drafting by having a rule that resolves ambiguity against their interests.

4.13 Reductio Ad Absurdum, the Camel's Nose, the Slippery Slope, the Parade of Horribles, and the Thin Entering Wedge

All the terms in the title refer to the same thing: the extension of a proposed principle to absurd or undesirable lengths. I will refer to them all as "reductio ad absurdam," because that is the most common term for the ploy. Law professors are the masters of reductio ad absurdum. They induce unsuspecting law students to espouse some proposition and then come up with increasingly absurd hypotheticals to show that the proposition is untenable. Try this with your friends, and they will soon be ex-friends. The proposition becomes untenable because it ultimately conflicts with another principle that is important to its proponent.

This ploy points out the consequences of generalization of an opponent's position. In this sense, reductio ad absurdam is based on an assumption of consistent treatment of like cases. It is an effective tool in the legal system where, as is addressed in greater detail in Chapter 5 below, consistency is a core systemic value.

For example, suppose that your opponent argues that it is obvious that people should not fly because they were not born with wings. You can point out in response that perhaps people also should not ride on bicycles or in cars, because they were not born with wheels. The generalized proposition is that people should not use modes of transport unless they were born with the relevant equipment. You are simply pointing out that the generalized proposition encompasses more than the speaker probably intended, and more than could possibly make sense.

From a negative perspective, reductio ad absurdam argues that if you adopt the threatened approach, or interpretation, or policy, you will need to apply the rule to restrict conduct in far more cases where it would be absurd or unappealing to do so. From a positive perspective (this is often called the camel's nose or the parade of horribles), it argues that if you allow the conduct at hand to go unrestricted, there will be a lot more such conduct. In this latter form, it may even be an argument about demonstration effects or incentive effects: once you drop your guard, you will have lots of similar cases, and they will destroy your position.

The most effective strategy in response to a camel's nose or slippery slope argument is to distinguish cases: to explain why the case at hand is different from the parade of horribles your opponent has conjured. You should anticipate the parade of horribles and make clear at the outset that your principle is limited to a reasonable range of cases that includes the case at hand. A bit of extensional pruning might be in order.

Another effective strategy is to point out that other similar types of distinctions have been made without the camel's nose, slippery slope, or parade of horribles coming to pass. We actually are in control of our destiny and must make nuanced and reasoned distinctions.

Point: If we accepted your principle, while the results would not be unacceptable in the case at hand, the result would be absurd, or horrible, in other cases where it might be extended.

Counterpoint: All things in moderation—there is no need for such an extension, and the absurd or horrible cases you posit are not before us.

Counter-counterpoint: But it is the principle of the thing; once we establish the principle that you argue for, we will not be able to hold back the absurd and the horrible.

5

Arguing From Precedent

An argument in which the advocate's desired outcome is consistent with past action is remarkably persuasive for a number of reasons. The reference to precedent has intrinsic appeal, insofar as consistency is a good thing. Consistency, where there is no good reason for inconsistency, is beneficial in order to promote predictability and to avoid the effects of bias. Consistency preempts challenges arguing that the decision seems to be based on the rule of men, not the rule of law.

We do not need a sophisticated, modern legal system to see the appeal of precedent. Imagine a primitive group of village elders faced with a problem or a dispute. Anthropologists report that they will often turn to precedent—how did we deal with this last time?—in order to determine how to deal with it this time. This is one of the reasons elders have these decision-making roles—they have greater knowledge of precedent than the younger generation. The wisdom of elders is, in part, based on experience.

Consistency also helps to economize on decision-making resources. Instead of "reinventing the wheel" every time, we just follow the way we did it last time. You can immediately see the value as well as the limitation there: we may have done it wrong last time, or times may have changed, so we should not just follow our prior decision.

The common law system has brought this consistency-based style of argument to its highest form, and so it is worthy of our study. Australia, Canada, Ghana, Hong Kong, India, Ireland, Israel, Jamaica, New Zealand, Pakistan, Singapore, Uganda, the United Kingdom, and the United States are some of the principal common law countries. Common law is a system that supplements legislative law with judge-made law. The judges don't actually legislate in the conventional sense, but their decisions in particular litigated cases are taken as binding precedent. This judge-made law may interpret statutes, or it may elaborate new rules from scratch, as in certain areas of contract, property, or tort. Civil law countries (most of the rest of the world, except for those following Islamic law, which also has a system for judge-made law) do not have a rule of binding precedent, but they also value consistency, so the differences in this regard are subtler than they may at first appear.

Also, note that judges who say (1) they will not engage in judicial legislation, and (2) they will respect existing precedent are saying something somewhat inconsistent: that they will respect prior judicial legislation but not engage in judicial legislation themselves. Their approach may be understood as conservative in the non-political sense: don't change anything. Alternatively, they may be understood as advocating a new rule of greater deference to legislatures, while also maintaining deference to prior judicial legislation.

Point: We should follow precedent.

Counterpoint:
i.   Yes, but the precedent you rely on is distinguishable from the present case.
ii. No, that precedent never made sense, or no longer does.

5.1 Consistency and Law

Recall Ralph Waldo Emerson's aphorism, "A foolish consistency is the hobgoblin of little minds." Well, consistency is the watchword of the law, so you might infer that lawyers have little minds. In order to avoid such inferences, and hobgoblins (good but troublesome fairies), let's put the emphasis on the word "foolish." So, to coin a phrase, sensible consistency is the watchword of the law. This is true for all legal systems, not just common law systems.

Indeed, if we are to follow John Quincy Adams' call for a government of laws and not of men, then consistency is required so that those laws mean the same thing every time they are applied. Otherwise, to the extent that the variation is controlled by men, it is a government of men. The very nature of a legal system, as opposed to a system of government by fiat of individuals, requires consistency. Lawyers may have little minds, but you may wish to join us in demanding consistency. Consistency is a bulwark against discrimination and corruption.

Arguments for consistency are founded in the very notion of a liberal democracy and are also founded in fairness. Inconsistency, by its nature, requires the treatment of one person worse than another. Some might say that we are not treating one person worse—we are just treating the other better. If that argument raises your suspicions, you are right: it is nonsense. This kind of statement may be made in connection with arguments about affirmative action: providing better treatment to members of disadvantaged groups. However, one cannot defend affirmative action by saying, falsely, that no one is treated worse—rather one must have a suitable rationale for different treatment.

Sensible consistency in the application of law is essential to a free society. But consistency is remarkably difficult to define. In order to determine what consistency means in particular situations, we must determine the basis for the rule, and for any exceptions to the rule. Consistency requires that a different treatment apply only where the rationale for the rule is inapplicable or the basis for an exception is applicable. It's all about determining the conditions for application of the rule: getting the "if-then" statement right.

Consistency of treatment is akin to non-discrimination. While we all may feel that we know discrimination when we see it, intuitively, there is a great deal of room for careful analysis. Is it discrimination to allow a person suffering from dyslexia extra time to answer questions on an exam? Is it discrimination *not* to do so? Or is it discrimination to fail to allow a person *not* suffering from dyslexia the same amount of time? Is it discrimination to charge a higher sales tax on cars that get worse gas mileage? What if opponents of the government in power own the company that makes the cars with worse gas mileage? How do you decide?

The same types of questions may be raised about the application of precedent. The core question is, as mentioned above, what does it mean to be consistent? The answer to that question depends on what the precedent is—what the "baseline" treatment is. We can look at prior cases and argue about what they mean in terms of the baseline. We are arguing, then, about the scope of the precedent and the basis for deciding the case, known in the legal lexicon as the *ratio decidendi*—Latin for the "rule of decision."

In the legal process in common law systems, courts formally seek consistency. In order to act consistently, they must first draw the essence, or find the ratio decidendi, from past decisions. And doing so often involves some discretion. So much for consistency. So much for the rule of law. Before we despair, we must recognize that the process of identifying the ratio decidendi is not so much, or at least is not completely, the responsibility of an individual judge. Rather, the essence is stated and restated in cases and commentaries, and by this statement and restatement it becomes more rigid. The legal process and the lawyer's professional training serve to guide or to constrain the decision by any particular judge. If everyone involved in a dispute understands how precedent is derived, and can appreciate how closely the judge follows precedent, then there are powerful social pressures on the judge to conform.

As I have stressed repeatedly, the law, like other rules, is by its nature incomplete. Within the legal system, we use the mechanism of interpretation, often carried out by courts, to complete it in particular cases—to determine how to apply it to particular cases. In order to apply the law consistently, it must be interpreted consistently. Incompleteness is a problem not just of statutes and contracts, but also of the common law. Indeed, we can understand the common law as a mechanism for incremental decentralized completion of incomplete legal rules.

Under our necessarily incomplete laws, it is not always easy to agree on what it means to be consistent. In effect, the laws are incomplete ex ante (when they are written, and before they are applied) because it is too costly, and in many cases impractical, to make them "more" complete. In order to determine whether the law is being applied consistently, we must identify the rationale for the interpretation in prior cases and determine whether it fits the current case.

Ex post—when it comes time to apply the laws—you can imagine that there are strong incentives for the parties in dispute to disagree on how the law should be completed. In a sense, what makes it possible to write laws is that we are to a degree unaware of the specific distributive outcome of writing the law. We do not yet know all the specifics of who will benefit and who will be harmed. Once we know, in a particular case, there is a lot more to argue about.

5.2 The Salience of Precedent

Lawyers, especially common law lawyers, like precedent, but so does everyone else. When faced with a new problem, it is not a bad thing to ask first, how did we deal with this issue the last time it arose? One rationale for this instinct is simply laziness, or, as some like to call it, the search for efficiency. The use of precedent is not just supported by a drive for sensible consistency but by a drive to economize on evaluation and decision-making. Of course, it may be that we fool ourselves by relying too much on precedent. It could be that if we thought the issue through again, we might come up with a better solution. But we might not, and we would have wasted all of that thinking time.

We can think of a body of recorded or remembered precedent as a vast storehouse of social knowledge—knowledge of how we dealt with these issues in the past. It can be a powerful argument that the treatment you propose is consistent with precedent, both in order to maintain a rule-of-law-based society and in order to benefit from earlier analysis. Some types of decisions will benefit from adherence to a principle of conservatism: the burden of proof is on those who seek change. This principle is expressed in the aphorism, "if it isn't broken, don't fix it." You might say that those who seek change must show that something is indeed "broken."

Moreover, it is not just the benefits of earlier analysis and conservatism that we obtain as a result of adherence to precedent. In addition, depending on the age of the precedent, and more importantly on how often it has been followed and how well accepted it appears to be in general society, we might assume that the precedent has a degree of support from consensus, or at least acquiescence. Perhaps, after the judge made the decision, opposing advocates tried to convince other judges to reverse it, or tried to have legislators amend the underlying law or pass a law to reverse it, and failed.

Adherence to precedent is not just about consistency or the rule of law. It is also about information and experience. In a number of pursuits, we say that there is no substitute for experience. Experience allows us to make nuanced decisions based on information gathered through practice. Businesses have long recognized that this type of know-how is valuable and should be captured, recorded, and disseminated. The common law represents a system for doing so.

There may be circumstances in which research or other non-experience-based information may be more useful, but there will definitely be circumstances in which experience trumps research. In a sense, the common law system may be viewed as an inductive, as opposed to deductive, method for determining social policy. It dates back as far as the Battle of Hastings in 1066.

So, we can envision the common law process—the process of accreting, and then according respect to, decisional experience—as a kind of evolutionary process. It is an experimental process in which principles may be announced and evaluated over time. The main question that we must ask of this type of process is whether its discriminating mechanism is a good one or not: does it recognize error and correct it?

The comparison to evolution depends on the quality of the selection mechanism. Darwinian evolution entails the survival of the fittest. We do not really have a theory of "survival of the best rules"—we even lack consensus on what would be "best." However, reasonable people might expect the crucible of time to tend towards revising "bad" precedents and respecting "good" ones. Judge Richard Posner famously argued in 1972 that the common law's discriminating principle was efficiency. While this has been debated inconclusively, it is to be hoped that judges would tend toward choosing the principles that they think are best for society, and this choice would certainly have something to do with efficiency.

In summary, precedent is powerful because sensible consistency is good, because it relies on earlier analysis, saving time and energy, because it is supported by the principle of conservatism, and because it may be supported by consensus or acquiescence. These rationales are often applicable outside the legal system as well. Thus, an argument that emphasizes the support of precedent may be very powerful indeed.

Consistency-based reasoning is everywhere, and so these arguments are relevant in all areas of life. In business, two employees might argue that they should get similar raises. Good human resources practice suggests that consistency of treatment is important, so it is necessary to determine the ratio decidendi for a differential raise. In fact, the very concept of "reasonableness" of treatment requires that we have a ratio decidendi—a reason—for treating two people differently in any situation. Sensible consistency is often an indicator of fairness and objectivity. Consider teachers grading papers or parents dealing with their children. It is good to be, and to be seen to be, consistent.

5.3 Rationes Decidendi: The Essence of Decisions

Beginning law students in common law countries that have rules of binding precedent, like the U.S., learn how to read judicial opinions in order to distill the ratio decidendi of these cases. They do so in order to know what the law is, because under binding precedent, once we define the precedent it is a rule of law.

The goal is to seek the narrowest rule of decision that will explain the outcome of the case. What is meant by "narrow" in this context? The explanation must explain the decision and nothing more. It does so in the form of an "if-then" statement, such as "if A, B, and C, then X." Here, you can see the room for debate. How do you know that it is not A and B, then X, or B and C, then X? Here, the decision-maker must articulate a reason why each of A, B, and C are necessary, and sufficient, conditions for X.

Point: We should follow the precedent set by a prior case.

Counterpoint: There are many distinctions between that case and this one—you cannot know that the factors that caused the decision in the prior case are all present in the current one.

Counter-counterpoint: Those are indeed distinctions—but they don't make a *difference*. The *salient* factors—the ones that make a difference—are the same.

Counter-counter-counterpoint: How do you know which are the salient factors?

Empirically, without actually getting into the mind of the judge, we really cannot tell from a single case which were the salient facts—the necessary conditions. The judge might tell us what she relied on, but we just don't know for sure. So, any time an opponent argues based on a single case as precedent, you know that he is on infirm ground.

Actually, the search for the ratio decidendi is guided by the principle of Occam's razor, which suggests that the simplest explanation of a phenomenon—the one that requires the fewest assumptions or conditions—is likely to be the correct one. Occam's razor is not a firm rule of logic, but a guide to decision-making under uncertainty. In a legal context, looking at a particular set of cases—we might compare cases to observations in science—the common threads that are both necessary and sufficient to explain all of the observations can be understood as the ratio decidendi.

With a series of cases, we may use Occam's razor to find the ratio decidendi that parsimoniously explains the entire series and nothing more. If we have a case in which A, B, and C are present, but other cases in which only A and B are present and still others in which only B and C are present, and the outcome of each case is X, then we know that B is necessary for X, but A and C are not. It could be that one of A *or* C must be present, but we just do not know from this series of cases.

To illustrate the discussion of A, B, and C, assume that we are talking about murder, and that A is intent to kill, B is action causing death, and C is death. In modern legal systems, all three are necessary to constitute murder, but you can imagine an alternate legal system in which intent is unnecessary or in which actual death is unnecessary.

Furthermore, there may be circumstances in which no single ratio decidendi can explain the series of cases. For example, if A and B, B and C, and A and C all result in X, then we do not know whether any of them is necessary or sufficient for X. The rule could be that any of those combinations result in X, but no other conditions result in X. Or it could be that the presence of any one of those factors results in X.

What if in one decision, A, B, and C result in X, and in another decision, A, B, and C result in not X? Then the one thing we know is that we have no clue as to what results in X. Perhaps there were other unobserved facts that made the difference; we must identify them. Otherwise, these cases are inconsistent, and something must give way.

I have been using symbols—A, B, and C—to show the logic used in determining the ratio decidendi. This phase of legal analysis—the analysis of precedent—can be simply formulated as follows. First, you must distill facts into variables: characterize the facts as As, Bs, and Cs. Second, through the Occam's razor type process, you must determine which conditions are necessary and sufficient for X. There may be sets of cases—data sets if you will—that do not allow you, or your opponent, to determine which conditions are necessary and sufficient. So be it—you can point this out in your opponent's argument and, subject to ethical constraints, elide it in yours. As we know, the common law analysis process seeks to derive "if-then" statements from various sets of facts linked with conclusions. This is not intellectual gymnastics, but it can be an intellectual marathon: grinding analytical persistence is often rewarded with victory.

Let's concretize the use of ratio decidendi further. Securities statutes are intended to protect investors in stocks and bonds from fraud, and do so by expanding the definition of "fraud" beyond its traditional common law-based bounds. Securities laws were intended to make it easier to claim fraud in connection with sales of securities. In common law systems, statutes can be definitively interpreted through case law, which can constitute binding precedent.

The elements of the crime of securities fraud under U.S. law are understood today to include (1) a material misrepresentation or omission of fact, (2) fraudulent intent (scienter), (3) a connection with the purchase or sale of a security, (4) reliance by the plaintiff on the facts presented, (5) economic loss, and (6) causation of the loss by the reliance. We will focus on item (4).

It has been observed that item (4) (reliance) might be difficult for plaintiffs who purchase stocks or bonds in the securities markets to prove. Many people fail to read the prospectus or other materials distributed, or they fail to create evidence that they actually relied on particular statements in the materials that turn out to be false.

In response, the regulators and courts developed the so-called "fraud on the market theory," which was adopted by the U.S. Supreme Court in 1988 in the case of *Basic v. Levinson*. This approach allows plaintiffs the benefit of a presumption that they relied upon allegedly fraudulent information, even where they were actually unaware of the fraudulent conduct at the time of the relevant transaction. In effect, the ratio decidendi of *Basic v. Levinson* was that although item (4) would still be required, it would be readily satisfied without any evidence of actual reliance. If you have the other five elements, and the defendant cannot find a way to rebut the presumption of reliance, you win your case.

The ratio decidendi is important in common law systems because of the rule of *stare decisis*, or binding precedent: judges are generally required to follow earlier decisions (except when they don't—more about this below). What does it mean to follow earlier decisions? Since each decision deals with a new factual setting, what must be followed is the ratio decidendi. Remember that the common law system prizes consistency.

The ratio decidendi concept is the way that we define consistency where each case has distinctions: it is a way of determining whether the distinctions are salient. Another way of saying this is that it is a way of determining whether the distinctions *make a difference*.

Much of legal argument is consumed with determining which rule should determine the treatment of a particular circumstance. In a common law system with diverse judges operating in a decentralized environment, addressing different types of fact situations, there are bound to be lots of different rationes decidendi. In an argument, it is up to each lawyer to select the ones that help him win, and argue for their application.

Indeed, I fear that this discussion might give you a false sense of the precision and scientific nature of the identification and application of precedent. Rather, there is great contention over what the precedents tell us. If you read just about any non-unanimous U.S. Supreme Court decision, you will see that very skilled justices, applying these techniques at the highest levels, are able to use precedent to justify sharply differing conclusions. Few would argue that the U.S. legal system is totally indeterminate and malleable, but there is significant flex in the system. However, you can use the techniques presented in this chapter to see which judges hew more closely to precedent and which ones seem to be acting more, shall we say, "creatively."

A good portion of the first year of a U.S. law school education is spent illustrating in excruciating detail how earlier precedents can be

"distinguished" from the current case: how to argue that the adverse precedents are inapplicable and how the benevolent precedents dominate the
treatment of the current case. This process is no more than reasoning by
analogy and arguing about bases for similarity. Indeed, it has much in common with the technique of framing: advocates argue about which precedent
is most analogous to the case at hand. The similarity of the current case to
the prior case depends on the ratio decidendi of the prior case and the extent to which that ratio decidendi is invoked in the current case.

Point: The present case is governed by the precedent
encapsulated in the ratio decidendi of a long line of
cases.

Counterpoint: No, the present case is distinguished
from that line of cases by salient facts and is governed
instead by the ratio decidendi of a different line of cases.

5.4 Obiter Dictum and Cheap Talk

A principle of conservatism suggests that you should not establish general
principles until you need to. When a court decides something it does not
yet need to, or articulates an opinion that is not logically necessary to its
disposition of the case, it is seen to be exceeding its mandate to decide
cases as it becomes necessary to do so. To enunciate a general rule that is
not necessary to decide the case at hand and to reconcile the decision with
prior cases, violates this principle. When it does, it is referred to in Latin
as an *obiter dictum*, an incidental remark.

The idea of obiter dictum is a requirement for judges to walk the walk,
not just talk the talk, when they engage in precedent-based judicial legislation. While judges often feel the need to be eloquent, and to speak of

high principles, it is the job of the case law analyst to ignore all that and try to focus on the facts and the resulting ratio decidendi.

In these situations, even though the judges' statements may be wise and compelling, lawyers tend to discount them in the common law process. They reject statements that may have been made by the earlier court, but that were not of the essence in the earlier court's *action*. For them, this type of statement is mere "cheap talk." Because the statement was not combined with action, the earlier court did not bear the full political and professional consequences of its statement. And so, the logic goes, its statement cannot be of the essence or part of the ratio decidendi.

More importantly, obiter dictum is not part of the ratio decidendi, so consistency of treatment does not require respect for this earlier *statement*—it is not part of the *treatment*. In fact, identifying obiter dictum is simply the converse of identifying the ratio decidendi: anything the decision-maker said that is not part of the ratio decidendi is obiter dictum.

Outside of the courtroom, thinking like a lawyer, this type of argument is suggestive that we must be careful about arguments from consistency. Are we interested in consistency of action or consistency of thought? So, you might respond to the argument "that is what we said last time this arose" with "but that is not what we did last time" or, "but what we said in that connection last time was irrelevant to what we did."

Point: The present case is governed by the precedent encapsulated in the ratio decidendi of a long line of cases.

Counterpoint: The alleged ratio decidendi that you propose was mere obiter dictum—it was not necessary to the decision of that case and so should not guide us now.

5.5 Exceptions that Swallow the Rule

Some social arrangements change quickly and some change slowly. For example, a law can be repealed, effective immediately, or it can be subjected to increasing exceptions that eventually, in retrospect, can be seen to have gutted the rule. Think of the U.S. Glass-Steagall Act enacted in 1933, which separated commercial banking from investment banking and other non-banking activities. It never was repealed, but over the years, it was eviscerated by a series of amendments culminating in the 1999 Graham-Leach-Bliley Act.

The same thing can be done, with less formality, with precedents. As new cases come up, with new characteristics, we can distinguish those cases until the cases that are excepted from the prior rule become a majority of what originally was thought covered. This is not necessarily a bad thing but rather a way in which rules can evolve organically to meet changing circumstances. They can evolve based on experience.

When a rule has enough exceptions, can we still call it a rule? In fact, at some point, one might say that this rule no longer has the coverage and integrity it once had, and that it is time to say a few kind words and inter the thing. It is said that the "exceptions have devoured the rule." This can be an effective argument when someone seeks to apply a rule to you, and it has no obvious exception that covers your case. In a strong sense, it is an argument from consistency. If the rule has been abrogated for most cases, is it fair to apply it to the remaining subjects?

Point: You have broken the rule.

Counterpoint: That rule is so tattered with exceptions that it no longer makes sense to apply it at all.

Counter-counterpoint: The fact that there are exceptions shows that we are still serious about applying the rule (this is a case in which the exception may indeed prove the rule).

5.6 Breaking Precedent

At some point, a lawyer will find it difficult to distinguish cases or to argue for an exception from precedent. In these situations, the argument from conservatism—from precedent—may be countered by an argument from innovation. No one would gainsay that these cases present new circumstances; all circumstances are new and have unique characteristics. The past never repeats itself precisely. You might even claim that these are new times, giving rise to a need to rethink and to craft new solutions. Stockbrokers periodically make these claims: we do not have to worry about long-standing principles of valuation or about precedents for market reversal because this is a "new economy" or a "new paradigm." This is the moment when you should grab your wallet.

There are a few notable cases of reversal of precedent in U.S. legal history. The greatest one was the 1954 decision in *Brown v. Board of Education*, where the U.S. Supreme Court said, despite earlier decisions holding that sending black and white children to separate schools could constitute equal treatment, it now saw that in this context, separation is starkly inconsistent with equality.

Point: All our precedents suggest that the law is against you, and there are no available bases for distinguishing the present case.

Counterpoint: It is time to change the rule; there is no reason to adhere to consistency with a foolish rule.

5.7 Passive Virtues and Passive Aggression: Not to Decide Is to Decide

"Passive virtues" is a term coined by the great U.S. constitutional law scholar Alexander Bickel in 1961 to refer, approvingly, to sneaky procedural tricks used by judges to avoid deciding cases. We addressed some of these, like ripeness doctrine, when we discussed procedure in Chapter 3. Why do I call them "sneaky?" Bickel's idea is that these approaches are somewhat discretionary, to be used not necessarily because of their ostensible rationale, or consistently, but in order to achieve the goal of passivity when passivity is indicated by other circumstances. The passive virtues include arguments that the matter is not yet "ripe" for adjudication, that it is "moot" or that there is not a real case or controversy, that the matter is not amenable to review, that the plaintiff lacks standing, or that the court lacks jurisdiction. The parental analog is the parent's incredibly frustrating "we'll see" response to a child's request.

Why would judges want to avoid deciding cases? Perhaps they do so because in some cases society does better by muddling through without establishing a clear rule. Perhaps they do so because if they decided, it would come out the "wrong" way from a public policy perspective. Perhaps they do so because they wish implicitly to refer the matter to a legislature, which can decide the issue with greater analytical resources and greater political legitimacy. Passivity is aligned with conservatism: avoid deciding a case where the facts of the case may require the development of a new rule.

Outside the law, we might say, again, "if it isn't broken, don't fix it." This aphorism, if it has any meaning beyond the tautological, suggests that existing circumstances may be superior to alternatives for reasons that we are unable to observe without extensive analysis. It is a principle of conservatism based on information economizing. We might even extend the aphorism with another: be careful to avoid "the cure that is worse than the disease." Not every problem is worth solving, at least not yet. So, there are circumstances in life when it is best not to decide. Your 10-year-old might ask for a cell phone, and you might respond, "I'll think about it." Or you might say, "Let's wait and see at your next birthday," or "Let's wait and see when my cell phone contract is up for renewal."

We don't really know whether avoiding a decision is a passive virtue or is instead passive aggression. This is captured in yet another common aphorism: "not to decide is to decide." If the judges use passive virtues to avoid deciding a case, someone loses who would have won if the judges had complied more fully with their responsibilities. In life, outside the law, refusal to decide when people have rights that are being denied amounts to continued denial.

5.8 Specificity and Delegation

Legislators and makers of contracts have many choices. Their laws and contracts will no doubt be incomplete, but the degree of incompleteness is a choice. Similar choices exist outside the legal system. For example, people who make rules for sports or other non-legal pursuits also have many choices. One type of choice is the level of specificity of the rules. The game of Ultimate (aka Frisbee) is governed by 10 brief rules, fitting on a single page, while professional basketball has 65 pages of rules.

By providing a high degree of specificity in the original rule, the legislator provides great predictability to the governed persons and less discretion to judges, referees, or other third-party decision-makers. When legislators create laws with less specificity, they may be uncertain how best to structure more specific rules, or it may be too costly in time and resources, or in political capital, to do so. However, after a period during which it can observe experience applying less specific laws, a legislator may decide to adopt the common law or to modify the common law in a more specific set of revised rules. The development of the common law process itself can be understood as a mechanism for providing greater specificity over time: with each new precedent we know more about how the rule works.

The choice between less or more specificity provides some practical challenges and opportunities for any rule-maker. The rule-maker need not provide a complete set of rules right away: it can begin with a set of principles or a set of basic rules. Then it can decide later, based on experience, what the next step should be. This way of thinking about specificity also reminds us that the judge's discretion is not unconstrained if the legislature can change the rules after seeing what the judge has done. In this way and to this extent, the judge is a supervised agent of the legislature. In this way, also, we can see it is inappropriate to criticize judges for "judicial legislation" when their function in this context is to fill in the gaps in general rules provided by the legislator.

Point: The judge has gone beyond the specific language of the statute, engaging in excessive and undemocratic judicial legislation. Alternatively, the referee has gone beyond the specific rules of the game.

Counterpoint: The judge or the referee is charged with making decisions. Where the law or the rules of the game are set in general terms, we can infer that the legislator or rule-maker implicitly delegated to the judge or referee discretion to fill in the details.

5.9 Citations, Footnotes, and the Pedigree of Information

In the context of arguments based on precedent, the footnotes contained in a written argument display the precedent and telegraph the quality of support for the author's position. Footnotes are the "put up or shut up" response to the critical epistemological question in any argument: how do you know?

Footnotes serve the role in argument that reproducibility serves in science: they allow others to see for themselves the basis for the author's statements. They also provide a research log or trail, disclosing to decision-makers and opponents the basis for the author's positions, and allowing the opponents to assess and seek to undermine that basis. Therefore, it is a strategic decision how much of the basis for your argument to disclose in the footnotes. The strategy depends on how important it is to make your initial affirmative case versus how important it is to make your opponent's rebuttal more difficult.

Lawyers have a love-hate relationship with footnotes. We fear that our reliance on footnotes shows up the lack of poetry in our souls. We fear that our reliance on footnotes means that we lack our own voices or bases for our statements: everything has to come from somewhere else.

And yet, there is something beautifully liberal, even selfless, about this requirement to support every assertion in our reasoned argument. The underlying principle seems to be that none of us is entitled, in the liberal world of law, to impose his evaluation on others. Instead, we must lead the other, by mustering and displaying information, by anchoring our arguments in precedents, laws, and facts, ineluctably but voluntarily, to come to the same conclusion. Once we understand the proper role of citations in displaying the basis for statements, it is difficult to criticize the modesty, and honesty, that footnotes evince.

Citations allow the reader to see, and to evaluate for himself, the quality of the support for the author's statements. The reader can see the pedigree of the information on which the author relies. It is possible for an author to build a great superstructure of argument on a slender base of authority. So, the reader must consider the support for the author's statements and may need to reverse engineer the author's logic a bit. The quality of support for a proposition will often be in the eye of the beholder. In addition, the reader needs to make sure that the integrated entirety of the supported points makes sense; this is the analysis and synthesis method of legal argument discussed earlier.

Point: Here is my argument, and each component is fully supported by the authorities cited in the footnotes.

Counterpoint: You win. I got nothing.

Alternative Counterpoint
i.   I shall examine each footnote and determine the degree of support supplied by the authorities cited. We'll see. (Note that each footnote might be the loose thread that, if pulled, can destroy the entire argument.)
ii. While each of your points is adequately supported, they do not together make a complete argument.

6

Arguing About Facts

Facts are facts, and lawyers have no special power over facts. But the appreciation of facts and the salience of facts in deciding a matter are the province of lawyers. Maybe that is why some lawyers become skilled investigators. Recall that in deriving the ratio decidendi of a prior case, and in determining the characteristics of a current case, it is necessary to taxonomize the facts: to place messy facts into discrete and meaningful categories.

Law professors sometimes make the following challenge to their students: "You let me control the facts, I'll let you control the law, and I will always win." The point is that every claim about the application of rules is dependent on the facts that support either compliance with or violation of the rules. Remember that each rule is an "if-then" statement: if certain elements are satisfied, then certain legal consequences ensue. The professor is saying that if she controls whether the "if" is ever satisfied, she controls whether or not the law applies.

As we discussed earlier, every legal claim is composed of a number of elements. Each of these elements is essentially dependent upon the appreciation of the facts in the case. In fact, this is the core of legal analysis: determine the elements of the claim, and then examine each element separately to determine whether each is satisfied. So, if the elements of the crime of murder are death, causation, and intentionality, we have three factual questions. If there is a defense available based on an argument that the defendant acted in self-defense, or lacked the intellectual capacity to appreciate or intend the crime, we have additional factual questions. Each of these questions may present a high level of complexity.

6.1 Determining the Salience of Facts

We do not know which rules apply until we know the facts. We do not know which facts are important until we know which rules apply. Breathe deeply; yes, it is circular. But that does not mean it is impossible. The art of reasoned persuasion is an iterative, recursive heuristic, meaning that we must go back and forth between the facts and the rules until we have a good fit. We cannot see the facts properly until we know what framework to place them into, and we cannot determine what framework to place them into until we see the basic contours of the facts. The great economist Friedrich Hayek said, "Without a theory, the facts are silent."

In the end, the critical arguments will be about whether a rule has been broken. Therefore, the final question will be whether the factual requirements to find that the relevant rule has been broken have been met. Where your formal argument is weak—where the formal analysis of the facts does not support your claim—it may be attractive to empha-size other facts that are informally appealing but not part of the formal claim. When your opponent emphasizes certain facts, you must determine whether those facts are part of the analysis or, alternatively, whether your opponent is "blowing smoke" or setting up a diversion.

Think about a claim by a multinational corporation (MC) against a low net worth individual (LNWI). Perhaps the MC claims that the LNWI damaged the MC's property and must now compensate the MC. The LNWI's lawyer may emphasize the disparity of power and resources. If you represent the MC, it is up to you to point out that the elements of a claim for property damage do not include the relative power or financial wherewithal of the parties. The LNWI's lawyer is seeking to reframe the case as one about distribution of power or wealth.

Point: Facts X, Y, and Z are the basis of my claim against you.

Counterpoint: In this type of case, X and Y are relevant, but Z is not. And without W, they are insufficient to complete a claim against me.

6.2 Evidence and Missing Links

Think of an apparently simple case of murder. We have video that shows the defendant pulling the trigger on a firearm aimed at the victim and the victim is mortally wounded. We have a corroborating eyewitness account. What must we know in order to determine that the defendant is guilty? First, can we rely on the video or eyewitness account? We know that video can be doctored, and individuals can lie or make mistakes. Outside of a courtroom, especially where the stakes may not be very high, we might tend to make assumptions that video is authentic and that the eyewitness account is true and correct. But there may be circumstances where it is useful to challenge these types of evidence. Second, did the victim die due to the wound? Did death ensue from the act of the defendant?

It is the advocate's job to examine carefully the factual components of his opponent's claim and to seek to cast doubt on how the facts are assembled to establish the opponent's claim. What are the missing links between the different facts? Where is there doubt about the facts or about the reliability of the evidence for the facts?

The evidence may become unreliable if your opponent cannot establish that it was gathered properly or preserved properly. Was it legal to video tape these events? We have a video of the defendant pulling the trigger, but how do we know the gun was loaded or the videotape was produced at the time the victim was shot? Are we sure there was not another shooter? How do we know the videotape was not subject to tampering later?

The evidence may be circumstantial, meaning in this context that while the evidence is consistent with your opponent's argument, other possible facts that do not indicate the defendant's responsibility are also consistent with your opponent's argument. Circumstantial evidence is good evidence, but it is not by itself conclusive evidence.

One of the essential functions of lawyers is to identify gaps like these in opponents' narratives and to highlight them. It takes a careful, imaginative, and suspicious turn of mind to do it well.

6.3 Causation of Harm and Negligence

Some causal links are easy to establish. If I pull the trigger and the gun fires, and the bullet from my gun hits you, and you die of blood loss from the wound caused by that bullet, no one would argue with the assertion that I've killed you. Other causal links are tougher to establish. One of the central areas in which law is different from ordinary experience is in its analysis of causation. In fact, law has critiqued and subverted common understandings and assumptions about causation.

The legal perspective on causation is easiest to see in relatively simple cases of tort or crime. A child runs after a ball into the street without looking and is struck by a car. Horrible. What caused the injury to the child? Who is responsible? Is it the child himself, the child's parents, the driver of the car, the thrower of the ball, the manufacturer of the car, or the designer of the street, or shall we blame this tragedy on the act of a cruel deity, leaving the child's parents with no recourse? You can readily see the circumstances under which any of these might be thought responsible, but we normally assign primary blame to the driver of the car.

If you focus on the child running into the street, it is easy to see that causation is in a sense reciprocal: if the child had not run into the street, there would be no harm; if the driver had stopped, there would be no harm. If the parent had monitored the child more carefully, there would be no harm. You can also see that, at some level, the causation of the harm is more a matter of social relations or public policy than a matter of scientific testing of cause and effect.

One type of question about causation is whether a person—in order to be found responsible—must be the sole cause, a sufficient cause when there are other contributing causal factors, a necessary cause, or a contributing but not sufficient cause. Sole causation means that the causal factor must be sufficient by itself to cause the relevant effect, and no other causal factors contributed. Sufficient causation means that even if other causal factors contributed, the causal factor in question was sufficient by itself to cause the effect. Necessary cause is sometimes referred to as "but-for causation," meaning that but for the causal factor, the result would not have ensued.

Different legal rules or social situations set different standards of responsibility. But outside the legal context, there is much room for debate on what constitutes a sufficient level of causation—in relative and absolute terms—to give rise to responsibility.

Point: You caused harm to me.

Counterpoint:
i.   My actions were only one factor—without the other factors, you would have experienced no harm.
ii. My actions may have contributed to the harm, but the other factors were sufficient by themselves to cause you harm.

Even science involves a good deal of social or political choice. One need only refer to early arguments about the existence or cause of global warming to bring to mind some of the difficulties. For a long time, cigarette companies were able to suppress scientific knowledge about the causal relationship between smoking and several diseases. The question of whether the residue of bovine growth hormones in meat causes cancer or other disease has bounced around quite a bit between the European Union and the United States. All these examples illustrate the plasticity, or at least the contestability, of science. This contestability is often reduced over time, as evidence and consensus grows. Does anyone doubt today that smoking cigarettes causes cancer?

6.4 Brandeis Briefs and Scientific Experts

More than a century ago, a young lawyer from Boston was confronted with the task of convincing the U.S. Supreme Court that when the U.S. Constitution guarantees all citizens equal protection under the law, equal does not actually mean equal (so much for plain meanings). The lawyer needed to convince the court that when the citizens are female, the protection must be greater than for males, at least when it comes to working in a laundry. Indeed, the argument was that "equal protection" means unequal treatment. In order to win his case, the lawyer needed to convince the Court that an Oregon law prohibiting women from working in any "mechanical establishment, or factory, or laundry" more than ten hours during any one day did not violate the rights of women.

What was the young lawyer to do? If he simply argued to the Court that, in his experience, women were delicate flowers requiring nurture and sunlight—rather than drudgery—then, although he might well have received wise nods of agreement from the nine elderly male justices he sought to convince, he risked the justices concluding that their wives and daughters might find such chauvinism offensive, and to avoid unpleasantness at home, the justices might be inclined to decide the case against his client. No, he needed to provide the justices with something other than personally-held beliefs on which the justices could hang their bowler hats when they returned to hearth and home.

The lawyer, Louis Brandeis, who eight years later would himself become a member of the Supreme Court, assembled all of the extant social science research on the detrimental impact of long work hours on the health of women.[15] As a result of this evidence, the Supreme Court upheld the Oregon law. This was one of the first instances where an advocate emphasized the law-in-action over the formalistic pronouncements of the law-in-the-books. The term "Brandeis brief" has come to refer to any use of policy-oriented extra-legal arguments in briefs.

Because statistical evidence is generally circumstantial evidence—it goes to correlation, rather than causation—it must be used carefully. But there are many areas, and they are increasing, in which the way we know things is through complex statistical analysis.

I was once a member of a university committee charged with evaluating whether a university researcher had engaged in scientific misconduct. The researcher had been required to make certain very precise measurements. The charge was that the researcher had fabricated some of the measurements. We had no way to go back and check the measurements: how could we know whether the numbers were real or fake?

The committee decided to check with a statistician. The statistician looked at the pattern of the final (smallest) digits of the measurements and compared the existing pattern with the expected random pattern. The result: there was an infinitesimally small chance that the existing pattern was random—that it occurred naturally. The pattern was damning evidence of a very high likelihood that the numbers were fabricated. The numbers were unlikely to have occurred naturally, and there was no other plausible explanation of the non-random results. Therefore, it was clear the standard of proof we were charged with applying—whether the preponderance of the evidence indicated scientific misconduct—was met. The chances of any cause other than fabrication were so small, that this evidence might have also satisfied a criminal standard of proof: proof beyond a reasonable doubt.

---

15 *See Muller v. Oregon*, 208 U.S. 412, 423 (1908).

Statistical evidence can be good circumstantial evidence, and circumstantial evidence can be very persuasive. Its persuasiveness depends on the likelihood of other causes being responsible for the phenomenon at issue.

Point: I have statistical evidence that use of your product is strongly correlated with harm, and we have tested and ruled out all conceivable alternative causes.

Counterpoint: That is only circumstantial evidence and cannot be accepted as proof of responsibility.

Counter-counterpoint: Circumstantial evidence is indeed not necessarily conclusive, but strong correlation, combined with careful evaluation and rejection of alternative causes, is highly suggestive.

Lawyers, and everyone else who wants to be able to make, evaluate, and oppose arguments about causal relationships, need to be conversant with statistical methods. These methods allow us to estimate the magnitude of correlations and even to estimate the relative causal impact of multiple causal factors. Where data can be obtained regarding large numbers of events, these methods can provide great insight into causal relationships. They can provide great insight both for application of law and for law reform.

6.5 Quality of Evidence: The Best Evidence Rule

Historians speak of primary sources and secondary sources, and they prefer primary sources consisting of physical evidence, photographs, other recordings, or first-hand accounts by current observers. Common law systems have long had a rule that secondary sources would not be accepted as evidence where primary sources are readily available. It is easy to see that any case or argument is made more persuasive if it is based on higher quality evidence, so, in a sense, this rule of evidence should be understood also as a rule of argument: always use the most persuasive evidence available, which will ordinarily be that provided by primary sources. If I am trying to prove that I own a parcel of real estate, the deed itself, perhaps combined with a check of the land registry, is the best evidence rather than my testimony or that of a neighbor or an observer.

Similarly, when your opponent attempts to support a proposition using secondary sources or other less reliable forms of evidence, this may be an indication that there is a weakness in his argument. Presumably, unless he is lazy, he would have provided the primary source were it available. So, as we have learned, we must evaluate the quality of support for each component of our opponent's argument. These components include not only the propositions of law but also the quality of evidence regarding factual matters. It is only through this grinding analysis that we can identify the loose threads. Once we see them, we can pull on them until the entire argument unravels.

6.6 Exclusion of Evidence

We noted in Chapter 1 that the legal system itself sets the rules about what kinds of arguments will be successful within that system. In fact, the legal system does more than that; it also limits the evidence that may be used to craft a persuasive argument—the parameters for the kind of knowledge it will take into account. Why would a decision-maker ever determine not to consider certain information? Is that not the definition of "ignorance"—to ignore knowledge?

Certain types of evidence may be excluded because they are known to be unreliable or easy to fabricate. Other types of evidence may be excluded in order to deter the gathering of that evidence: in the U.S., evidence obtained by illegal search is generally excluded from use in criminal trials.

As parents, as executives, and as citizens, it is not uncommon to receive information that was improperly obtained. One employee might hack another's email account and anonymously provide evidence of impropriety. A classified document might be illegally divulged to Wikileaks. The recipient is often in a quandary about what to do with this information. For the same reason that illegally obtained evidence is excluded in criminal prosecutions, you might decide to ignore this type of evidence in non-legal disputes. On the other hand, evidence is evidence, legal rights are legal rights, and a crime is a crime. In situations that involve wrongly acquired evidence, we see another conflict between a specific type of procedural justice—avoiding the use of improperly obtained information—and substantive justice.

Point: The evidence proves my case.

Counterpoint: The key piece of evidence is inadmissible and so cannot be considered as part of your case.

6.7 Estoppel: Blocking Argument

Estoppel literally means to "bottle-up" or prevent, and it prevents parties from arguing or asserting certain facts. Often, estoppel is related to the idea of reliance. If the counter-party relied on the first party's statement of facts or acquiescence in a particular situation, the first party is estopped from asserting otherwise. The first party is blocked from claiming facts inconsistent with its earlier explicit or implicit statement.

You might wonder why any argument or assertion would be foreclosed? Isn't this another form of ignorance? The main idea here seems to be reliance and repose: once you have had a chance to make a statement or to correct a misunderstanding, you are thereafter estopped from doing so.

One important example of estoppel is in the law of letters of credit. Letters of credit are important mechanisms for making payment and for financing. Once the beneficiary of a letter of credit demands payment, if the bank that issued the letter of credit accepts the demand or waits more than the specified number of days, the bank may be estopped from claiming that the beneficiary did not properly satisfy all the conditions for payment.

The rule of estoppel in this context has two purposes. First, estoppel allows the beneficiary to rely on the bank's acceptance of the demand for payment or on the specified passage of time, which might be construed as acquiescence. Second, it discourages banks from trying to find problems in the beneficiary's demand for payment should the bank communicate with its customer (on whose behalf it issued the letter of credit) and learn that the customer was dissatisfied with the beneficiary's goods and preferred not to pay for those goods.

You can no doubt think of many interpersonal circumstances where you are informally estopped in the sense that you can no longer assert a fact or an argument. In fact, you may think of circumstances in which you have sought to get someone's "sign-off" or "buy-in" early so that they would be blocked from complaining later. This process is used in connection with negotiation of contracts or other legal documents. A business agreement or treaty will be circulated for comments. If you fail to make your comment at the appropriate time, you will at least be criticized for raising an issue after everyone (rightfully) assumed it was settled. This is a procedural criticism: your comment is no longer timely.

Point: I have fundamental concerns about our project.

Counterpoint: The process that we have been following allowed opportunities to make this point and you did not do so in the allotted time. It is too late.

6.8 Presumptions: Shifting the Burden of Proof

Presumptions serve a number of different, and substantive, functions. First, a presumption against the person likely to have control of the evidence can force that person to produce the evidence. After all, if the presumption is against you, and you have evidence that can rebut the presumption, you have incentives to present it. Second, under uncertainty, a presumption may allocate responsibility where it is most likely to lie. It may be useful to make a presumption if, after investigation, it is better than flipping a coin between two otherwise equally plausible inferences.

Abraham Lincoln, a great lawyer as well as a great President, was fond of asking, "If you call a tail a leg, how many legs does a dog have?" When his victim would innocently answer "five," he would reply that the victim had it wrong: "Calling a tail a leg does not make it a leg." Making a presumption does not make the fact presumed so.

In Charles Dickens' Oliver Twist, Mr. Brownlow convincingly accuses Mrs. Bumble of theft, and Mr. Bumble hopes to keep his job but is confronted with a presumption. The dialog is as follows:

"It was all Mrs. Bumble. She would do it," urged Mr. Bumble; first looking round to ascertain that his partner had left the room.

"That is no excuse," replied Mr. Brownlow. "You were present on the occasion of the destruction of these trinkets, and indeed are the more guilty of the two, in the eye of the law; for the law supposes that your wife acts under your direction."

"If the law supposes that," said Mr. Bumble, squeezing his hat emphatically in both hands, "the law is a ass—a idiot. If that's the eye of the law, the law is a bachelor; and the worst I wish the law is, that his eye may be opened by experience—by experience."

The Oliver Twist story is an excellent example of a presumption used as a device for allocating responsibility. The law presumed that a wife acts under a husband's direction in order to allocate responsibility to husbands to supervise their wives. But it is not strict liability in the sense that husbands are not liable for the acts of their wives no matter what. Rather, the husbands are presumed responsible and must bear the burden of proving that they are not in fact responsible. The presumption shifts the burden of proof from a complainant to show that the husband is actually responsible for his wife's acts, to the husband to show that he is actually not responsible. This presumption may have made sense under circumstances where husbands controlled the family wealth, and wives were effectively "judgment-proof" because they held no assets of their own. In this sense, Bumble's objection that the law is an ass is beside the point: it is not important whether the presumption comports with reality or not. Indeed, it need not even be a good approximation of reality; the idea of the presumption is to shift the burden of proof.

Point: The law, or society, makes a presumption regarding facts, and based on that presumption, you are assigned responsibility.

Counterpoint: That presumption is not based in reality: there are many circumstances in which it cannot be expected to be true.

Counter-counterpoint: Presumptions need not be based in reality, but may still be appropriate in order to transfer the burden of proof.

7

Rhetorical Tricks

Rhetorical tricks use language in ways that can further an argument but can also be seen as dishonest, or at least disingenuous. I relate them not to prepare you to use them, but to prepare you to counter them—consider this chapter in the vein of "defense against the dark arts." You will no doubt avoid using sophistry to make the weaker argument appear the stronger, but your opponent may not be so principled.

These rhetorical tricks are seen both inside and outside a legal setting. Most rhetorical tricks prey on sloppy thinking or passive acceptance. Therefore, critical thinking and tough questioning (is that really so? how do you know?) can reveal and contradict any of these tricks. By learning the structure of these tricks, you will be able to identify and rebut them.

Formal logic, scientific method, and statistical analysis are all formidable defenses against these rhetorical tricks. Moreover, once you reveal the weak logic in one of an opponent's arguments, you can capitalize on it to cast doubt on her other arguments. (This strategy itself relies on an error of composition—incorrect inference from a part to the whole—but it can be persuasive.)

7.1 Non Sequitur: That Doesn't Follow . . .

Non sequiturs may be observed in arguments about facts and in arguments about law. *Non sequitur* is a term for a whole class of circumstances where the asserted predicate does not indicate the desired conclusion, but the speaker acts as though it does. Therefore, several of the other rhetorical tricks identified in this chapter can also be understood as non sequiturs.

One example of a non sequitur is where an advocate argues that because something is covered in a contract, all similar items are covered. So, if a lease contract prohibits the lessee from keeping dogs and cats on the leasehold premises, it does not follow that snakes are also forbidden. (I see your non sequitur and raise you an expressio unius.)

You may use a non sequitur to persuade an audience despite the logical fallacy of the non sequitur and, indeed, because the non sequitur may mask the logical fallacy. For example, in the famous murder trial of the former football star O.J. Simpson, a glove was found at the crime scene. Its match was found at Simpson's estate. The gloves contained DNA evidence from Simpson and the victims. The glove from the crime scene had been soaked in blood, and police had frozen and unfrozen it several times. The prosecutor, goaded by Simpson's lawyer, Johnnie Cochran, asked Simpson to try on the glove from the crime scene in court, and it seemed too tight for Simpson. In his closing remarks, Cochran repeated, "If it doesn't fit, you must acquit." There was lots of alternative evidence of guilt, and there were possible extraneous reasons why Simpson had trouble putting the glove on in court. For one, Simpson tried it on over rubber gloves. Nevertheless, Cochran was able to focus the jury's attention on whether the glove fit, as opposed to whether there was proof of guilt beyond a reasonable doubt. Non sequiturs are a way of focusing attention away from the salient facts and on a fact that may be true but is not salient.

Point: The elements of this crime are A, B, and C. Each element has been proven beyond a reasonable doubt. You must convict.

Counterpoint: The prosecution has failed to prove D.

Counter-counterpoint: D is not salient to this case: it need not be proven in order to constitute the crime of which the defendant stands accused.

7.2 Ad Hominem Arguments: Discrediting the Source

No matter what criticism we level at the source of information, we cannot necessarily infer from this criticism that the information provided is false. Even a broken clock tells the correct time twice a day. Ad hominem attacks are those that seek to discredit the source of information, without addressing whether the information is reliable or not.

On the other hand, it is not an inappropriate ad hominem attack if we show that the speaker is dishonest, depending on the nexus between the evidence of dishonesty and the matter at hand. There are few among us who have always avoided dishonesty. Perhaps you have been a dinner guest and have falsely complimented the host's cooking, or the behavior of the host's children, or the beauty of the host's interior decorating. The fact that we have been dishonest at times does not necessarily do much to impugn our current statements.

Thus, an ad hominem attack is a type of non sequitur—an irrelevancy with the focus on the speaker's credentials. An inappropriate ad hominem attack occurs when the nature of the criticism of the speaker has nothing to do with the truth of the information provided by the speaker. For example, if the speaker is a visual witness to a murder that took place some distance away, it is generally appropriate, if true, to claim that the speaker is nearsighted and was not wearing corrective lenses at the time. But it is an inappropriate ad hominem attack to point out that the speaker is a pacifist or a politician.

In legal proceedings regarding complex matters, expert witnesses are often useful. It is appropriate to impeach an expert witness on the basis not only of the quality of the witness's expertise and preparation but also on the basis of apparent bias. For example, if the expert witness has appeared many times in similar matters, always on the same side, opposing counsel may point out that this expert witness appears to have a bias and may even have been hired in consideration of the bias.

Of course, there is an opposite kind of stratagem: hiding one's true biases in order to appear neutral and influence the opinion of others. One type of stratagem along these lines is sometimes known as an "AstroTurf" strategy, because it is a synthetic "grass roots" campaign where the interest group seeks to appear to have broad public support, but in actuality it is funded and otherwise supported by a particular business or political sponsor.

Point: My expert opinion is that the defendant took inadequate care to prevent the injuries that the plaintiff sustained.

Counterpoint: You are a socialist.

Counter-counterpoint: My political perspective, religion, nationality, or sexual orientation are all irrelevant to my expert opinion, which is based on the application of a special methodology and years of experience.

7.3 Fallacies of Causation: Post Hoc Ergo Propter Hoc, Affirming the Consequent, Correlation Versus Causation, and Omitted Variable Bias

Scientists and social scientists are the experts in determining the links between cause and effect. One fallacy that they seek vigorously to avoid is the confusion of correlation with causation. *Cum hoc ergo propter hoc* is when two things occur together and one is assumed to cause the other. *Post hoc ergo propter hoc* is when the alleged cause precedes the alleged effect. This type of confusion can be illustrated with an old joke. A man walking down Broadway in Manhattan comes across an old friend who is stamping his feet and shouting, "No peanut butter!" The first man asks what is going on. The second explains, "This keeps away the elephants." The first responds, "There are no elephants in Manhattan." The second responds, "See, it works!" Clearly, the fact that there is correlation between stamping and shouting, on the one hand, and the absence of elephants, on the other, does not prove causation.

One variety of post hoc ergo propter hoc is known as the fallacy of "affirming the consequent." An "if-then" statement has an antecedent (if) and a consequent (then). If the if-then statement is true, every time there is an antecedent, there will be a consequent. But it will not necessarily be true that every time there is a consequent there is also an antecedent—other causes might result in the consequent.

Affirming the Consequent:

i.   *If she is a lawyer, then she is expert in the law.*

ii. *She is expert in the law.*

iii. *Therefore, she is a lawyer.*

You can readily see that expertise in law does not necessarily constitute someone a lawyer. Many politicians, journalists, judges, and scholars become experts in the law without becoming lawyers.

The category of evidence that lawyers label "circumstantial" suffers from the same type of problem: it fails to provide a basis for inferring causation from correlation. If we observe a man driving a car that was previously stolen, this does not mean that he stole the car. Similarly, the fact that a man is *not* driving the car does not mean that he did not steal the car. Driving the car is neither a necessary nor a sufficient basis for inferring that the man stole the car. While circumstantial evidence may be logically insufficient, an accumulation of different types of circumstantial evidence may be sufficient in ordinary experience, and even in court, to prove causation. For instance, if we find the victim's blood on a suspect's shoes, if the suspect owned the murder weapon, and if the suspect had a strong motivation, reasonable people might conclude that the suspect is guilty. Each of these facts by itself is circumstantial evidence.

Circumstantial evidence is related to the problem referred to by statisticians and scientists as "omitted variable bias." We cannot infer causation from correlation, because there may be an alternative causal variable that has not been included in our analysis, perhaps even one that causes both the alleged cause and the illegal effect. Or it may be that the causal relationship is reversed: the alleged effect actually results in the alleged cause. The tighter the correlation is and the less plausible the alternatives are, the greater our comfort in inferring causation.

Point: People who smoke cigarettes develop lung cancer at a much greater rate than people who do not.

Counterpoint: Correlation is not causation; for example, it may be that people who smoke tend to work in jobs with greater workplace air pollutants. We just do not know.

Counter-counterpoint: No, correlation is not necessarily proof of causation, but once we exclude other causes, correlation provides pretty persuasive evidence. In other words, once we control for all the things that might plausibly cause lung cancer, like workplace air pollutants, if the correlation persists, we have a good idea what is going on.

7.4 Inappropriate Inference from Limited Data

Be careful with rhetorical tricks that relate to statistics. Many times people use them in their arguments, and they can, in many ways, be misleading. Lies, damn lies, and so on. Most lawyers and laypersons do not have the expertise of a trained statistician. But we are all advised to think critically about the statistical inferences that we present or that are presented to us. (74% of statistics used in argumentation are made up on the spot.)

Without knowledge of statistics, a lawyer might assert that a particular medicine caused heart disease because nine out of ten patients who took the medicine developed heart disease. But a statistician might respond that ten patients is too small a sample from which to draw reliable conclusions. Furthermore, we must know more about the sample—how many of them would have developed heart disease without the medicine? Perhaps the medicine is used as a last-ditch effort to forestall heart disease, given only to those who will certainly develop heart disease without it, and the good news is that it is effective in one of ten patients. The lawyer should know about the rules of inference in the science of statistics in order to be able to support his argument or at least to anticipate criticisms.

7.5 Occam's Razor and the Exception That Proves the Rule

As discussed in Chapter 5, Occam's razor is a tool for identifying and refuting your opponent's suggested inferences. It is more a rhetorical defense than a rhetorical trick. Occam's razor, otherwise known as the rule of parsimony, says we should not seek out complicated explanations when simple ones are available, provided that the simpler ones also account for the facts. In formal terms, it holds that if there is an explanation of a phenomenon that requires fewer exceptions or assumptions than another, we should be drawn to the one that requires fewer. This is not always correct—the more complex explanation may indeed be the correct one—but the main point is that we do not have any reason to be attracted to the more complex explanation.

> *Medical diagnostics is guided by the following version of Occam's razor: If you hear hoofbeats, think horses, not zebras. In diagnosis as in other areas, it often pays to "keep it simple, stupid."*

Occam's razor is not formally a tool of legal analysis, and, in fact, it is more often seen as a tool of logic or science than of law, but it is a useful general tool of analysis and argument that definitely has application in legal contexts. As mentioned in our discussion of precedent, it is the best tool for distinguishing ratione decidendi from obiter dicta.

Going back to our suspect who owns the murder weapon, has a motivation, and has shoes spattered with the victim's blood, we could make assumptions that someone stole or borrowed the weapon, had his own motivation, and deviously sprinkled the victim's blood on the suspect's shoes. And while all these things are possible—and if there were evidence that they occurred or existed it would be important—without such evidence the better inference is that the original suspect is the murderer. Whether or not his guilt is proven beyond a reasonable doubt depends on your definition (or a jury's or judge's definition) of a reasonable doubt. But the simpler explanation is more attractive than the more complex explanation that requires us to explain more "exceptional" phenomena.

In practical terms, despite the fact that guilt in a criminal case must be proven beyond a reasonable doubt, and the prosecutor always bears the burden of proof, we might say that the proponent of the more complex explanation of a phenomenon often informally or implicitly bears something like a burden of proof. If there is a lot of good circumstantial evidence, and the defendant has a separate, arcane, and implausible explanation for each one, judges will implicitly ask whether it is possible that all these strange coincidences occurred in the same case.

If your alibi is that space aliens abducted you at the time of the crime, you should at least be able to produce some evidence to support your proposition, like alien artifacts. If you were observed at the scene of the crime, it will not be helpful to argue that the space aliens might have constructed a robotic double, which must have committed the crime. If the victim's blood is found on your shoes, it could be true that your dog bit the victim the day before without you becoming aware of the bite and drooled the blood onto your shoes, but the chances of the aliens and dog being responsible for all these facts are too small to constitute a reasonable doubt. Occam's razor points us to the simple explanation: you killed the victim.

Point: I have come to conclusion X because it provides the most straightforward explanation of the facts.

Counterpoint: I have provided alternative explanations that point to conclusion Y.

Counter-counterpoint: Yes, but your explanations require me to assume that a lot of unexpected and implausible circumstances occurred—I'm going to go with the simple explanation.

A somewhat different, and more hospitable, approach to exceptions is contained in the expression "the exception that proves the rule." This expression, of course, is nonsense: exceptions do not prove a rule, but only disprove it, unless the rule is modified to contain an appropriate exception. Whenever your opponent says "that is the exception that proves the rule," you know that you've got him cornered, because he probably has given little thought to the way the exception actually disproves the rule or why the rule should be understood as valid despite the exception. He's really just pleading with you to ignore the exception.

7.6 When Did You Stop Beating Your Wife? Embedding Assumptions in Questions

It is sometimes possible to sneak an assumption into an argument by embedding the assumption in a question or in an unrelated statement. If this rhetorical ploy goes unnoticed, then the assumption goes unchallenged. In the television courtroom crime drama, when the lawyer does this to the defendant on the witness stand, the jury lets out a collective gasp, and it is time to cut to a commercial.

Point: At what point did you decide to monopolize the market for personal computer operating systems?

Counterpoint: I never decided to monopolize the market for personal computer operating systems, so I cannot answer the question as posed. Nice try.

8

Arguing About Substantive Responsibility

Although this book is not intended to address substantive legal rules broadly, some substantive legal rules or doctrines are fundamental to the way lawyers think and argue. Moreover, these substantive legal rules go to the core of arguments about responsibility, and can be useful in all sorts of situations.

8.1 The Reasonable Person and Due Diligence

Despite Freud's successful proposition that each of us is greatly influenced by the irrational, lawyers and legislators share an affinity for a fiction known as the "reasonable person." The reasonable person standard is referenced, either explicitly or implicitly, in many legal rules. The idea is that if you conform your behavior to that of the reasonable person, you should be insulated from liability.

In tort law—the law of civil liability for harms—the reasonable person standard is used as a standard of care in common law systems: if you acted with the probity of a reasonable person, you will not be found negligent and will therefore not be liable for the harm to others that ensued. You might understand it as an incentive to suppress your irrational tendencies.

The next question, of course, is how do we know what a reasonable person would do? The reasonable person standard is, to a large extent, defined only in the eye of the beholder, and the authoritative beholder is the judge or jury in a trial. There will be easy cases and hard cases. Easy cases involve the drunk driver speeding at 90 miles per hour against traffic on a highway. Hard cases are when someone comes into your home and trips over your rug.

In order to be a reasonable person, you should engage in a risk assessment of your acts. A full risk assessment would look like a risk-adjusted cost-benefit analysis, examining (a) the probability of the risk eventuating, (b) the magnitude of harm if the risk eventuates, (c) the benefits of the action that entails the risk, and (d) the availability and cost of less risky alternative measures. In effect, you are required to act reasonably and to value the risk of harm to others as you would value the risk of harm to yourself: a risk-adjusted "golden rule." An economist would look at this approach with approval—you may satisfy the reasonable person standard if the aggregate risk-adjusted social benefits exceed the social costs. But this is cold comfort to the person who bears the social costs.

Point: Your action resulted in harm to me, and therefore you should compensate me.

Counterpoint: I acted with the care of a "reasonable person," and therefore I am not responsible for harms that ensued to you.

Counter-counterpoint: Nevertheless, it is unfair to force me to bear the costs of your action.

A similar "reasonable person" concept applies in a wide variety of business law settings, although it got its start in U.S. securities law—law relating to the sales of stocks and bonds. This is the concept of "due diligence," which applies a reasonable person standard to the quality of investigation by certain persons involved in a securities transaction. Within the context of public offerings of securities, if the members of the company's board of directors, or if the bankers facilitating the sale, conduct an investigation of the facts disclosed to buyers that satisfies the standards of due diligence, then they are insulated from liability under the securities laws even if those facts turn out to be untrue or incomplete. A due diligence investigation is one that follows the standard of care that a reasonable person would use in his own investment affairs.

The due diligence term is now used widely beyond the securities law field, both in other legal fields and in business. In business, it refers to an appropriately careful investigation. The core idea is that if you did your due diligence no one can criticize you for failure. This type of reasonable person standard allows each of us to act and to feel confident that if we meet the reasonable person standard, we will not be subjected to effective criticism. If the standard of investigation is approved in advance, all the better—those who approved the scope of investigation will be estopped from criticizing it, even if the harm it was intended to avoid eventuates.

Point: You were in charge of preparing for and implementing this corporate acquisition, and it has turned out terribly, costing us lots of money.

Counterpoint: I did an effective due diligence investigation, and my investigation did not reveal any of the issues that caused the problems.

Counter-counterpoint: An effective investigation would have identified all of the issues that could *possibly* have caused significant problems.

8.2 Exceptional Circumstances: Force Majeure

Law is all about rules and exceptions. However, it can be difficult to distinguish an exception from a rule. The exception may simply be another rule that conflicts with the first. As a result, much of legal argument is about the scope of applicability of rules—whether they were intended to apply to the case at hand. Another large portion of legal argument deals with the question of whether the case at hand is so exceptional as to be excluded from the operation of the rule. Lawyers often argue about what to do when one rule conflicts with another—does one rule provide an exception from the operation of the other?

Perhaps the most famous case along these lines is that of the trespasser under duress. Consider the possibility of a sailor, caught unexpectedly in a storm, tying his vessel to a stranger's dock without permission. The owner of the dock sues for trespass: unauthorized entry on the owner's premises. Is the general rule against trespass applicable to persons under duress? Is the case of a ship at sea in a storm so exceptional as to be excluded from the operation of the trespass rule? If not, is there an exception for persons under duress?

Is there a difference between the inapplicability of a rule and an exception from the rule? What about an orthogonal rule, which seems to mandate or permit an action prohibited by the first rule? Perhaps there is not a difference for laypersons, or in logic, but lawyers may care about which is the rule and which is the exception because it may make a difference for the allocation of burdens of proof and persuasion. Usually the complainant has the obligation of proving the principal case, while the respondent has the burden of proving any exception.

Coming back to our sailor, is there a limitation in the scope of the rule against trespass, is there an exception to the rule against trespass, or is there a countervailing rule that those in distress have a right to take shelter reasonably in another's property, and does this right to shelter overcome the rule against trespass? We have raised three formal possibilities: inapplicability of the rule, an exception from the rule, and a conflicting rule that supervenes the first rule. These formal legal possibilities would have analogs in non-legal discourse about the propriety of a sailor using a stranger's dock in a storm.

Similar questions about rules and exceptions arise where two parties enter into a contract, and one promises a specified performance. What happens if something subsequently happens, causing the promised performance to become impossible, much more costly, illegal, or useless to the promisee? These are the legal doctrines of impossibility, impracticability, illegality, and frustration. "Impossibility" means that performance has become literally or practically impossible. "Impracticability" means that it is more practically impossible, or too costly. "Illegality" in this context means that the law, it turns out, prohibits the performance. "Frustration" means that the performance by the promisor is no longer useful to the promisee.

Depending on the legal system involved, and depending on whether your contract has a clause that specifies what to do if these types of occurrences arise, if the acts required by the contract become impossible, impracticable, or illegal, performance by the promisor might be excused. This would implicitly place the burden of the occurrence arising on the promisee—the person owed the performance. The idea of frustration is that the reason why the promisee wanted the promisor to perform the requisite act no longer exists. So, if I hired a personal hairdresser for a term of ten years, and immediately became bald, I might argue that the contract was frustrated.

These types of exceptional-circumstance cases are illustrations of the problem of incompleteness in the law: in statutes, in case law, and in contracts. This problem of incompleteness can be addressed by greater completion: by writing force majeure clauses that can direct how these types of cases shall be resolved. A force majeure clause specifies different types of events that may occur and directs how these events shall be handled.

Alternatively, the problem of incompleteness can be addressed by reference to adjudication. But the adjudicator needs principles by which to resolve the case. In a sense, if the adjudicator is given specific instructions, then the laws and contracts are completed by these precise instructions. Where the adjudicator is given more general instructions, we can still say that the laws or contracts are completed, but the adjudicator has a greater role to play and perhaps greater discretion.

Point: Your contractual obligation is clear—you must perform it.

Counterpoint: Even though the contract does not provide an explicit exception were performance of my obligation to become impossible or impractical, generally applicable law does. So, my performance is excused.

Counter-counterpoint: By stating your obligation in a clear and unqualified way, our contract was intended to place the burden of problems that might arise squarely on your shoulders.

8.3 Form Versus Substance

Like a parent who makes rules for her children, the legal system is constantly trying to set rules and to make sure that the regulated person does not find loopholes. Nowhere is this problem more endemic than in the U.S. tax system. Tax collectors try to set tax rules to differentiate between different types of circumstances, and taxpayers immediately structure their affairs to try to take advantage of low-tax treatment.

For example, if there is a lower capital gains rate, compared to the rate of tax on ordinary income, taxpayers try to restructure their income as capital gains instead of ordinary income. How can they do this? Recently, in the U.S., hedge fund managers have structured their compensation as a "carried interest," in which they receive a share of the investment, which they argue is a capital asset producing capital gain rather than ordinary income as compensation for their services. For another example, instead of accepting an ordinary income royalty for licensing the use of a patent, the inventor of the technology might seek to sell the patent in the form of a capital asset, or place the patent in a corporation and sell the shares of stock of the corporation. The tax collector might attack this, piercing through the formal arrangements to find the ordinary income substance.

Unfortunately, the decision whether to respect form, or to look through the form to the substance, is often made in unpredictable ways. This "form versus substance" debate brings us back to some of our discussions of interpretation earlier in the book: do we follow the simple text of the law or contract, or do we interpret or apply it so as to effect its purposes, or so as to give it effet utile? But what does the principle of effet utile counsel: does it argue that we should give effect to the loopholes, or does it argue that we should interpret the law so as to give it useful effect in taxation? If we extend the law beyond its text, are we engaging in judicial legislation, or are we violating the principle of expressio unius?

The form versus substance debate is often a result of the under-inclusiveness of the actual wording of the rule set forth in the law or contract. The argument to have substance prevail is an argument to remedy the perceived under-inclusiveness. However, it is not necessarily appropriate to assume that the law or rule is under-inclusive, or to put it another way, the under-inclusiveness might have been intentional. That is, it might have been intended not to cover the additional class of acts that are now argued to be covered by the substance of the rule. This seems entirely plausible in the area of tax, where lobbyists may have worked very hard to obtain loopholes to the formal application of the tax.

Point: My actions comply with the word of the law

Counterpoint: But they violate the spirit of the law.

Counter-counterpoint: But the greater spirit of the law is the rule of law, under which the law prohibits only those acts that are covered by the actual words of the law.

8.4 Law Versus Equity

The "law versus equity" debate is the converse of the "form versus sub-stance" debate. In addition to the formal legal rules sometimes leaving loopholes—being under-inclusive—legal rules can also include an error of over-inclusiveness. Remember that all laws and all contracts are incom-plete in their ability to specify what is to be addressed and what is not. This incompleteness can take the form of under-inclusiveness, but it can just as easily take the form of over-inclusiveness.

The rule can be written too broadly and therefore have unintended, or even absurd, consequences. Recall the rule of interpretation that man-dates that we avoid absurdity. The Bolognian rule against "spilling blood" in the streets seemed to prevent medical care, such as it was. In the com-mon law system, the concept of "equity" was developed in order to modify the formal law to relieve over-inclusiveness.

The history of the division and reunification of law and equity is worth recounting briefly. The early common law system that was developed in England was viewed as being, at times, hyper-formalist, with the result that it got some things "wrong"—the results were unintended or absurd. It was understood that the courts were the representatives of the king, and so it was recognized that individuals could petition the king for redress where the application of the strict letter of the law by the courts resulted in what the petitioner felt was inequitable. As this petitioning became institutionalized, specialized courts of "equity" were developed to determine whether redress should be available. Over time, the equity function has been merged back into the courts of law, but the idea continues to be to relieve the burdens of strict formal application of law.

> **Point:** My actions comply with the spirit of the law, and it would be inequitable to apply the formal law to me.
>
> **Counterpoint:** But they violate the letter of the law.
>
> **Counter-counterpoint:** The application of the law should be constrained so that the law is not applied inequitably.

You can readily see how this type of letter versus spirit argument would play out in all sorts of situations where there are rules: employment, sports, and school, among others.

8.5 Rights Versus Duties: Noses Versus Fists

The great judge Oliver Wendell Holmes observed that "The right to swing my fist ends where the other man's nose begins."

What if you put your nose somewhere that it does not belong? To put it another way, does your right to swing your nose end where the other man's fist begins? To state this simply, and generally, we might say that my rights end at your rights. That, of course, sharpens the conflict and makes its resolution less obvious: does the nose always get priority over the fist? Often, arguments involve multiple conflicting rights. Sometimes, my vision of my right seems to go beyond your nose.

The possibility of a conflict among rights is easy to see in arguments in the U.S. about abortion, where rights of others are argued to go considerably beyond a woman's nose. Here, we have a conflict between rights of the fetus to develop into a child and live, rights of the mother to determine whether she will carry the fetus to term, rights of the father or potential grandparents over the same issue, and rights of others in society to avoid funding abortions. There are rights, or what some see as alleged rights, everywhere, and they conflict with one another.

Without taking sides, let's look at the debate about whether Catholic hospitals may be required to provide to their employees health insurance that includes coverage of the costs of contraception, including abortion-inducing drugs. Under an Obama administration policy, religious organizations are not required to pay these directly, but the insurance companies are required to cover them for "free," and you can be sure that the insurance companies will find ways to cover their costs in the fees that they charge their clients. If we consider substance rather than form, the services are not free. So, to keep this simple, let's cut through these complex facts by assuming without further evaluation that money paid by Catholic hospitals for their employees' health insurance is fungible, that at least indirectly, the Catholic hospitals are paying something for contraception services to their employees, and that these services include abortion.

Rights-talk definitely becomes indeterminate to settle the debate. First, Catholics (and others) feel strongly about the right to life of the fetus. Second, the Supreme Court of the United States has found that a woman's right to determine whether to have an abortion is a constitutionally-protected privacy right. (Some hope that this precedent will be overturned.) Third, the Catholic hospitals argue that they have a collective right to freedom of religion that prevents government from ordering them to provide insurance that indirectly pays for abortions. Fourth, under U.S. law, the employees of the hospital have a right to health insurance that includes coverage of contraception.

My main point is that there are rights everywhere, and that simply calling something a right does not end the argument. Just about everything I want can be argued to be an alleged "right." But more surprisingly, just about everything you want can be argued to be inconsistent with an alleged right of mine. The problem with rights-talk is that it can cut off a discussion too quickly: rights seem indivisible and not subject to compromise. Furthermore, many rights-based arguments can be met with a reciprocal rights-based argument.

Consider this in a family context. Few of us who are parents of teenagers have not thought we had a right to expect our teenager to comply with some obligation, only to hear the response: "I have a right to decide for myself."

Point: I have a right to decide.

Counterpoint: Your decision interferes with my rights.

Counter-counterpoint: My right is superior to yours.

Notice how it is often possible for rights to be reciprocal: it is possible to meet a claim of right with a claim of an opposing right.

If you have a right to something, we ordinarily think that someone else has a duty to provide it to you, whether it is the state or private persons. Further, that "someone else" might see this duty as inconsistent with a right of theirs: yes, once we begin to argue about rights and duties, it's a mess.

Let's say your opponent says that he has a right to something, and let's say for a moment that you concede your opponent's right. This does not mean that you necessarily have a duty correlating to your opponent's right. This can be quite important in areas of so-called positive rights, like the right to health or the right to sustenance or shelter. We may well concede that each person has these rights, but the question is who owes any particular person the correlative duty. For the rights mentioned, usually we think of the state of which the person is a citizen as the obligor.

The issue of whether a right is appropriately matched by a duty might also come up in a contractual setting. Say you have a contract with company A, under which company A agrees to construct a factory. You have a right against company A, and it has a duty to you. Assume further that company A becomes bankrupt or is otherwise unable to carry out its duties. Do you have a right against the shareholders or parent company of company A? Probably not, even though you may feel that they are implicitly responsible for the obligations of company A. Unless you are careful, you may have a right, but no one capable of satisfying your right may have a duty.

Point: I have a right to X.

Counterpoint: You may well have a right to X, but I do not have a duty to provide it.

Counter-counterpoint: Unless you provide it, it will not be fulfilled. A right implies a correlative duty to fulfill the right.

Counter-counter-counterpoint: Not my problem.

8.6 Conflicting Values

There are few circumstances in the world of law and public policy that are unambiguous. In fact, at the center of all argument about law is the question of how do different rules—and through them different social values—relate to one another.

Here is a well-known example. We are interested as a society in ensuring that those who have committed a crime are punished. We are also interested as a society in ensuring that those accused of a crime are accorded fair treatment, including due process of law. But protecting the principle of punishment may not be consistent at all times with protecting the principle of fair treatment. In the U.S., as discussed earlier, courts have developed an exclusionary rule that bars consideration of evidence that is obtained through measures that violate certain rules of due process. This rule holds despite the fact that the violation of the rules of due process does not affect the veracity or relevance of the evidence. The judicial goal or value is to provide disincentives for future violations of these rules of due process.

All legal discourse touches upon conflicts of our values. We as individuals, we as a society, or we as a group of people party to a contract, have many values that become built into our laws and agreements over the course of time.

We may agree in advance with differing degrees of specificity how to sort out the values, but value conflicts come up in unexpected ways, or they might come up in expected ways, but still occasion argument. As I stated in Chapter 3, part of legal creativity is the ability to see disputes in new ways, invoking values that might not have been seen at the outset.

9

Who Knows What Lurks in the Minds of Lawyers?

Legal training includes the analytical and argumentative methods described in this book. Based on this training, and based on legal thinking, legal methods, and substantive legal rules, lawyers may exhibit some behavioral traits that seem, well, unusual. In many ways, these traits are also useful tools of argument that are honed through experience, though they do not fit neatly into any of the other categories used in the book. I include them here so that new lawyers and non-lawyers can identify them in relevant situations, and utilize them as needed. These ideas represent important "folk wisdom" of the best lawyers.

The training lawyers get, and the experiences they have, contribute to the way that they think, and it is not possible to turn off these ways of thinking at will. As Justice Oliver Wendell Holmes famously said, "the mind, once expanded to the dimensions of larger ideas, never returns to its original size."

9.1 Being a Lawyer Means Never Wanting to Say You're Sorry

While each of us knows that an apology can salvage a relationship, pre-empt the urge for revenge, or precipitate forgiveness, lawyers often have a different view. Lawyers are afraid that an apology might be understood as an admission of guilt or responsibility, under circumstances where guilt or responsibility might not otherwise be found. This does not mean that we—lawyers and non-lawyers alike—should never apologize. It does mean that there is an additional consideration that should be addressed prior to making an apology.

Perhaps even more perversely, lawyers often fear that fixing a dangerous condition might be viewed as an admission of its danger. In response to this conundrum, rules of evidence in many countries, including the U.S., prevent the introduction of repairs of dangerous conditions as evidence of danger. Not that it isn't interesting evidence, but the incentives would be all wrong.

Point: Why don't you apologize for your negligence, and fix the condition that caused the harm to me?

Counterpoint: I admit no wrongdoing.

Counter-counterpoint: I hereby agree that your apology and repairs will not be considered evidence of wrongdoing. At least one of us is an adult.

9.2 Words, Words, Words: Context, Precision, and Wiggle Room

For lawyers, a word can have one meaning in one context and another meaning in another context. For example, in the summer of 2012, the U.S. Supreme Court decided a case about the constitutionality of the central provision of President Obama's signature legislative achievement: an individual health care mandate. In order to examine the law under rules about jurisdiction, the Supreme Court found that the individual health care mandate was not a tax. Then, in order to uphold the law, the Supreme Court found that it was. To some extent, this is a legitimate implication of the fact that we always interpret words in context, but in this case, context-based interpretation is inconsistent with the interpretive principle of effet utile—under which we assume that use of the same words would generally mean the same thing.

Lawyers are "symbolic analysts." They use words as symbols, not just as language with integrity and grace. Sometimes, in order to do justice to the words, or to attain maximum clarity, it is necessary to do a bit of violence to the language. It is certainly disruptive if legal rules or judicial decisions try to be literary at the expense of precision. Often, there is a best way to express a specific concept, because all the alternative ways of expressing it lose an important element of precision. If we depart from that best way in order to provide a more beautiful expression, or even in order to avoid repetitiveness or prolixity, we lose precision. A professional should never do that, and when you are working in a context in which you care about the precision of your commitments and those of others, you should not either.

"Polonius: What do you read, my lord?

Hamlet: Words, words, words.

Polonius [aside]: Though this be madness, yet there is method in't."

William Shakespeare, Hamlet, Act II, Scene ii

Legal words are most useful when they have an optimal degree of precision. There are cases in which the optimal degree of precision is not the maximum degree of precision: we may want to leave some discretion to a judge or other decision-maker. But where we want maximum precision, our words should be like plumbing: there should be no leakage of meaning. There should be no room for our opponent to wiggle out of his commitments through extensional pruning.

Lawyers are expert at using words with precision, but conversely, they are also expert at using words with ambiguity. For a long time (until I became more mature), I delighted in responding to a dinner host's offer of a dish that I did not relish with the following line: "I would like nothing better." Do you see the reason for my childish glee? But more seriously, constructive ambiguity can allow people to move forward and can preserve wiggle room for your client.

9.3 Possession is Nine Tenths of the Law, and the Facetious Golden Rule

Lawyers understand, perhaps better than others, the costs of argument and of using the legal system. Lawyers also understand that burdens of proof are often allocated to the plaintiff or the one seeking a change in the status quo. This seems to be the source of the aphorism "possession is nine tenths of the law." It is also part of the basis for a facetious "golden rule" of law and finance: he who has the gold makes the rules.

If I possess an asset—it could be real property or personal property—and you claim it, you have to incur the costs of litigation. While you can impose on me the costs of defending that litigation, you must be able to bear your own costs, unless we are in a legal system that awards costs to the successful litigant. Furthermore, burdens of proof will often favor the defendant because the plaintiff is generally assigned the initial burden of making a case. Therefore, he who claims an asset in another's possession has an uphill battle to fight: possession is nine tenths of the law.

The facetious golden rule that he who has the gold makes the rules is especially salient in finance. While the bank has its money—and before it lends to the borrower—the bank may make the rules. It may dictate the terms of the loan agreement, subject only to competitive pressures imposed by the presence of other banks and other sources of financing. Once the bank has made the loan, the borrower is in a much more powerful position. Although within an effective legal system, the borrower may not make the rules in the sense of changing the terms of the loan agreement, it is now for the bank to make and enforce a claim in order to get its money back. Possession is nine tenths of the law, and he who has the gold makes the rules. These elements of folk wisdom crystallize an important set of insights about how legal systems work.

9.4 Trees Falling in the Woods: The Importance of Observation and Evidence

For a lawyer, unless there is observable and admissible evidence of the existence of a thing or phenomenon, it does not exist. This way of thinking is not, or not just, because lawyers are faithless skeptics. Rather, it is because lawyers understand that legal systems and social argumentation depend on third-party knowledge: on the ability to provide evidence to third party decision-makers.

Generally, the defendant knows what he or she did. Often, the complainant knows more than third parties about what happened. However, both the defendant and the plaintiff are interested parties, and so, human nature being what it is, we tend to distrust their accounts.

In criminal cases, lawyers will listen carefully to the testimony of the victim, but it will also be necessary to obtain corroborating evidence. So, lawyers study how to appreciate evidence, how to obtain evidence, what types of evidence may be subject to limited admissibility in court, and how much evidence will be sufficient to prove a point. The same types of questions arise in non-legal settings: how and what types of evidence will be sufficient to prove a point? How do we as individuals and as a society determine what types of information or evidence are sufficient to establish a reliable inference? Our questions are answered by the rules of inference: the consensus standards about how we know things.

9.5 Oral Agreements are Not Worth the Paper They Are Printed On

The main problem with oral agreements is evidentiary. You should not accept an oral agreement if you may need to enforce it judicially or by referring the matter to a third party decision-maker. This is because your counter-party may deny its existence or dispute its contents. If you may need to rely on an agreement in the future, get it in writing. As a promisee, you are better off with a written agreement because its existence and contents can be physically shown to others, including courts. The ancient Chinese saying states, "faintest ink over sharpest memory."

There is a second problem with oral agreements, depending on the applicable law. In order to avoid arguments by purported promisees that an alleged promisor made an oral agreement, many legal systems make it a rule to decline to enforce certain types of oral agreements.

As a promisor, you still need to be careful about oral agreements. First, you may feel ethically bound by your oral agreement, or your community or business standing may be jeopardized if you do not comply with your oral agreement. Second, oral agreements, assuming they can be proven, may be binding in some legal systems.

9.6 Who Knows What Evil Lurks in the Heart of Man? The Lawyer Knows

Lawyers invented the prenuptial agreement. In anticipation of a blessed union of two individuals, based on love and with visions of familial intimacy and everlasting solidarity, the lawyer plays skeptic. This posture is not confined to marriage. Lawyers serve as the voice of skepticism in all sorts of transactions, be they loan agreements, joint venture agreements, or sales contracts. Lawyers are experts in fights. The lawyer asks, "What happens if this is all a failure, what happens if it turns out that you are defrauding me, what happens if there is a nuclear disaster?"

> *"Pessimism is only the name that men of weak nerve give to wisdom."*
>
> **Mark Twain**

Does nature or nurture produce this skepticism? Who knows—but this skepticism has a very useful function in ensuring that potentially complex relationships operate smoothly, efficiently, and fairly. Certainly, in a transactional setting, clients may come to rely on the lawyer to address all the details of the transaction. These details include both actual issues and what we might call "contingent issues." Actual issues include, for example, questions of whether a merger transaction will trigger defaults under loan agreements or whether the acquiring company will become responsible for the retiree medical obligations of the acquired company.

Contingent issues might include whether the acquiring corporation would be responsible if the products of the acquired company sold before the acquisition turn out to cause harm to customers or others after the acquisition. The contingent issues won't necessarily be a problem, but they might be. As mentioned earlier, the lawyer is also the one who should be on guard for potential extensional pruning.

9.7 Ass-u-me Makes an Ass of You and Me

Or, as Mark Twain put it, "It ain't what you don't know that gets you into trouble. It's what you know for sure that just ain't so." Lawyers try to be careful about what they assume. Careful analysis requires careful scrutiny of underlying assumptions.

The rules of logic include the most basic syllogisms, which are themselves based on factual knowledge about the world. For example, we may decide that we know (in fact, we assume) that goods that are located on a person's property are in the possession of that person. Then, the syllogism is (a) goods located on a person's property are in the possession of that person; (b) cocaine was found on your property; therefore, (c) you possess cocaine. The accuracy of this syllogism is dependent on the accuracy of its predicate assumption that we can infer possession from location.

In preparing for an argument, the careful lawyer will examine the opponent's chain of syllogisms and determine the level of support for each link. Where there is a weak link of assumption without knowledge, the lawyer will exert pressure.

9.8 Credibility Counts: In Law and In Life

In many legal situations, the goal is to persuade a third-party decision-maker in connection with a dispute between two disputants. In the context of a trial, whether criminal or civil, an experienced lawyer will never lose sight of the crucial importance of maintaining the judge's trust in his credibility and that of his witnesses. If a decision-maker concludes that a witness is not to be believed with regard to one matter, then, human nature being what it is, the decision-maker will view the remainder of the witness's testimony through a lens of heightened skepticism, if not insurmountable disbelief.

> "The secret of acting is sincerity. If you can fake that, you've got it made."
>
> **George Burns**

The best attorneys—the cream of the persuasive crop—also recognize that the credibility of the legal advocate is itself crucially important. If a lawyer loses the trust of a decision-maker in one dispute, the lawyer's ability to persuade that decision-maker in subsequent disputes will be compromised. This is the lesson of the story of "The Boy Who Cried Wolf." Furthermore, decision-makers, be they judges, bosses, or prospective partners, *do* talk to one another. One of their favorite topics of discussion is the reputation in the community of the legal advocate for telling the truth.

Ethical considerations aside, if you hope to be a persuasive advocate for your own interests or the interests of others, lying to win the argument in which you are currently engaged is not worth the price of losing one's reputation for truthfulness. Accordingly, your clients, whether you are a lawyer with clients or a layperson representing your company, your community, or others, should recognize that there may be a tradeoff between maximizing their interests and maintaining your credibility. This is a conflict of interest they will have to accept. After all, they benefit in the current dispute from the credibility you have developed in prior matters.

> *Winning at all costs can be too costly. This particular argument may be part of a bigger decision, or part of a bigger set of decisions. It is important to preserve credibility by using the tools of argumentation responsibly, so that they will remain effective in your hands.*

10

Winning Arguments With Reasoned Persuasion

The lawyer's professional vocation is to argue about rules, agreements, and responsibility. But all of us argue about rules, agreements, and responsibility all the time as amateurs. We have seen in this short book that the analytical skills and arguments developed within the legal system provide powerful tools that can help us understand the world, make decisions, allocate responsibility, argue about the meaning of words, and win! While they often come cloaked in Latin phrases, or in technical jargon, legal techniques of argument are applicable to the way we advocate, negotiate, and resolve conflicts in everyday life. It is fortunate that these tools are not difficult to use. Here is what I hope you have learned.

Rules are always articulated in words, which always leave gaps and ambiguities. Indeed, all expressions of rules are naturally incomplete. The role of the legal system is to determine how to complete the rules, and thus how to apply them, in particular circumstances. There are many ways in which rules can be interpreted, and the canons of interpretation catalogued in the book can be deployed strategically to result in the desired outcome. One of the lawyer's jobs is to be suspicious of the possibility that opponents will engage in extensional pruning in order to evade their

responsibilities. Lawyers police extensional pruning when preparing contracts and when preparing laws. More broadly, they look for loopholes.

Legal argument, dispassionate in nature, is based on reasoned persuasion, and the reasoning is based on the legal analytical technique. This
analytical technique always involves determining what rules apply. As we
have seen, this is often uncertain and contentious. There is always room
for argument, either about the effects of competing rules or about the intended scope of the proposed rule. There is also room for innovation—for
identification of rules that might not obviously or conventionally be seen
as applicable but that may be implicated by the observed facts. Creative
lawyers will avoid prematurely categorizing a claim as one type of claim
or another but will be open to different categorizations. Strategic lawyers
will seek to frame their claims in a way that maximizes their chances of
winning.

Whether the rule comes from a contract, a statute, or a treaty, it can
always be broken down into a basic "if-then" statement. In this way, we
ask, what are the factual elements that give rise to liability under this rule?
Once we know these elements, the legal analytical technique is simply to
evaluate the facts in order to determine whether each element is satisfied.
In a planning context, prior to action, this method of analysis may reveal
a way to modify behavior in order to avoid the application of a restrictive
rule.

Consistency is essential to a legal system, indeed to the rule of law,
to fundamental fairness, and to a free society. Nonetheless, it is not always obvious what consistency requires. In order to determine whether
an action is consistent with precedent, we must determine the ratio decidendi—the essence—of the precedent. This is done by analyzing the
precedents into "if-then" statements, determining the elements that were
consistently required to be satisfied in the "if" component, and using those
elements to decide the case at hand. Occam's razor can help us figure out
which elements were consistently required. Understanding the importance of consistency also helps us understand ways we can best argue for
change. Occam's razor is also useful for evaluating facts, and suggests that

we prefer the inference that requires the fewest assumptions—the one that is the simplest is the most likely.

At the core of the vocation of law is recognition that procedural rules are important, both strategically and substantively. Strategically, we know that the choice of procedural rule, such as burden of proof, statute of limitations, or standing requirements, can determine whether one wins or loses in a dispute. Substantively, we know that any decision can be attacked on the basis of the procedure by which the decision is made. It is this sensibility that makes lawyers good managers. Lawyers learn to suppress their biases and reflexes in order to follow an appropriate procedure that will be reliable and that will be seen to be legitimate. Lawyers recognize that procedural justice is a real value, and that it can outweigh a sense of substantive justice. This recognition is essential to the rule of law and to a liberal society.

I hope that you will continue to learn, practice and use these legally-grounded techniques to develop your own art of reasoned persuasion with goals to illuminate, to speak truth to power, and otherwise to do good.

Glossary

A

Ad hominem argument. An attack on a speaker based on personal characteristics of the speaker that are irrelevant to the matter at hand and to the speaker's credentials.

Adjudication. The legal process of deciding a dispute that generally results in a judicial decision or sentence.

Administrative agency. A unit of the government with legal authority to administer and carry out the implementation of laws and regulations in a specific area.

Applicable law. The formal rules applicable to particular facts.

B

Binding precedent. In common law systems, the judge-made rule of law derived from earlier judicial decisions, which is binding in future disputes.

Brandeis brief. Any use of policy-oriented data in legal argumentation.

British rule of interpretation. A rule of interpretation under which contracts and statutes should not be construed in such a way as to result in absurdity.

Burden of proof. In formal legal proceedings, the obligation, allocated to one side or the other, to present evidence supporting a particular proposition. The allocation is often determined by reference to whether the matter at issue is one of the elements of an affirmative case brought by a plaintiff or prosecutor, in which case the burden is on the plaintiff or prosecutor, or is instead an element of a defense that may be brought by a defendant, in which case the burden is on the defendant.

C

Causation. In the legal context, the standard for determining whether a particular action caused a particular effect.

Cause of action. A legal basis for a claim.

Choice of law. In the context of private law, the selection of the law applicable to a relationship or dispute.

Circumstantial evidence. Evidence that is correlated to a particular legal finding, such as guilt or liability, but does not necessarily establish guilt or liability.

Civil law countries. Countries that have a European continental style legal system, which, for example, do not have a formal rule of binding precedent.

Civil lawsuit. A lawsuit between private parties, as contrasted with a criminal case.

Class action. A civil court procedure under which one party, or a group of parties, sue as representatives of a larger group of people.

Clear statement rule. A rule of interpretation to the effect that the court will not interpret a statute as violating a core principle or as contradicting an earlier statute, unless the legislature expresses its intent to do so explicitly and clearly.

Collateral estoppel. Doctrine holding that, if on the way to a final judgment there was a sub-issue that was definitively decided, then that sub-issue cannot be litigated again.

Common law. A legal system that supplements legislative law with judge-made law. *See **Binding precedent**.*

Conflict of interest. A circumstance where a decision-maker, such as a judge, has a special personal interest in the outcome of the decision.

Contingency fees. A way of calculating legal fees in which plaintiffs are able to compensate lawyers from a share of the recovery and where payment is contingent upon success.

Courts. Agents of the state authorized and empowered by the state to decide specified cases and to mete out punishment or remedies, as appropriate.

D

Default rule. A legal rule that applies automatically unless there are special circumstances, such as a contractual agreement to apply a different rule.

Double jeopardy. Criminal law doctrine that prevents a defendant being tried twice for the same crime.

Due diligence. An investigation that follows the standard of care that a reasonable person would use in his or her own affairs.

Due process of law. In the U.S., under constitutional principles, the requirement to provide fair process to defendants and others who are subject to legal proceedings.

E

Effet utile. French for "useful effect," effet utile is an assumption that is made in interpretation that each word and phrase has some meaning or purpose.

E.g. An abbreviation for the Latin words exempli gratia, which mean "for the sake of example."

Ejusdem generis. A canon of interpretation that provides that, when a general word or phrase is accompanied by a list of specific persons or things, the general word or phrase will be interpreted to include only persons or things of the same type as those listed.

Estoppel. A doctrine under which parties are prevented from arguing or asserting certain facts.

Expressio unius. A canon of interpretation meaning that the express mention of particular things of a certain type excludes all others of that type. It recognizes that positive statements can serve as the basis for negative inferences.

Extensional pruning. Initial use of words in the sense of their commonly accepted meaning and subsequent switch to a narrower definition in order to avoid obligations or refutation.

F

Force majeure. Exceptional circumstance that can provide a basis on which to excuse an obligation.

Forum selection clause. A clause in a contract that specifies the court or other tribunal that will hear and decide any dispute between the parties.

Forum-shopping. The selection of the court that will hear a case on the basis of the likelihood of a favorable judgment.

I

I.e. An abbreviation of the Latin phrase id est, which means "that is." It is intended to introduce a paraphrase or explanation of a previously stated category.

In pari delictus. The principle that one joint wrongdoer cannot sue another for damages that resulted from their shared wrongdoing.

Integration or merger clause. A contractual clause in which it is stated that the contract itself is the total and exclusive expression of the agreement between the parties.

J

Judicial review. A judicial procedure under which a law is reviewed by a court in order to determine whether it is constitutional, or under which the decision of an administrative agency is reviewed in order to determine whether it is consistent with law.

Jurisdiction. The power and scope of application of legal rules and legal processes.

L

Law. Formal rules that carry the sanction of the state.

Legal system. All the written and unwritten procedural rules that are applied to guide the determination and application of the law.

Lex specialis rule. This rule states that when faced with a conflict between rules, the one that applies more specifically to the facts should dominate the one that is more general. Also applies in private contracts, where the agreement has two contradictory provisions.

Liberal system. A democratic rule-of-law-based system of government.

N

Negligence. A type of cause of action based on allegations that the defendant failed to satisfy the applicable standard of careful action.

Non sequitur. A term for a whole class of circumstances where the asserted predicate does not indicate the desired conclusion, but the speaker acts as though it does.

O

Obiter dictum. The enunciation of a general principle that is not necessary to decide the case at hand and to reconcile the decision with prior cases.

Objective intent. The intent of a statute or contract that we can reasonably infer from objective evidence.

Occam's razor. Otherwise known as the rule of parsimony, a principle that holds that we should not seek out complicated explanations when simple ones are available, provided that the simpler ones also account for the facts. In formal terms, it holds that if there is an explanation of a phenomenon that requires fewer exceptions or assumptions, and one that requires more, we should be drawn to the one that requires fewer.

Original intent. The argument that we should understand a text's meaning as the parties originally understood it.

P

Parol evidence rule. A rule holding that if two parties make a contract, and if they demonstrate the intent that the contract is the final and complete statement of their relationship, no prior or subsequent additional communication, whether written or oral, can be used to show a modification or a different meaning of the contract.

Passive virtues. A term coined by Alexander Bickel in 1961 to refer, approvingly, to procedural devices used by judges to avoid deciding cases.

Positive law. The law as legislated.

Post hoc ergo propter hoc. The logical fallacy that because a certain factor precedes a specified occurrence, the factor causes the occurrence.

Precedent. A precedent is an earlier decision that is asserted to be similar enough to determine the outcome of the current argument under a rule of consistency, or binding precedent.

Prescription. Civil law analog of statute of limitation.

Presumption. A rule that, if certain facts exist, certain other facts will be deemed to exist.

R

Ratio decidendi. Latin for the "rule of decision." The goal of common law case analysis is to determine the ratio decidendi on which prior decisions are based.

Reductio ad absurdum. The extension of a proposed principle to absurd or undesirable lengths.

Regulation. Agency-made formal rules.

Res judicata. Rule under which once a case is finally decided (after appeals are exhausted), it cannot be heard again.

Ripeness. The requirement that in order to decide a dispute, it must first reach an appropriate stage. For example, it may be required that the complainant experience an actual harm before the complainant's claims become ripe.

Rule of lenity. Rule of interpretation holding that a vague criminal statute should be construed in favor of the defendant.

S

Standard of proof. The level of certainty of proof required to reach a legal decision. For example, in order to convict a criminal defendant in the U.S., there must be proof beyond a reasonable doubt.

Standing. The right to bring a lawsuit with respect to a specific matter.

Stare decisis. *See* **Binding precedent**.

Statute of limitation. Rule under which, after a specified period of time, claims can no longer be brought.

Substantive law. The part of the law that establishes specific substantive rights and duties, as opposed to the part of the law concerned with procedure.

T

Tort. A civil (non-criminal) wrong that can be the basis for a lawsuit.

Treaty. An international agreement between two or more states under which international legal obligations arise.

Tribunal. A court or other legally authorized body responsible for dispute resolution.

Tu quoque. A defense that holds that the accuser is himself guilty of a similar or other disqualifying act.

V

Voir dire. In jury trials, the process in which lawyers have an opportunity to try to identify bias of prospective jurors.

W

Whereas clauses, preamble, or lead-in: Language in a contract or statutory provision that is not intended to be binding but is intended as background and explanation for the binding obligations, often useful in interpretation.

Made in the USA
San Bernardino, CA
04 December 2016